ESTABLISHING THE CONVERTS

Books by Arthur C. Archibald
NEW TESTAMENT EVANGELISM
ESTABLISHING THE CONVERTS

ESTABLISHING THE CONVERTS

*What Pastors and Church Members Can
Do to Conserve the Results of Their
Evangelistic Efforts*

By ARTHUR C. ARCHIBALD

With a Foreword by
Dores Robinson Sharpe

———

PHILADELPHIA
THE JUDSON PRESS

CHICAGO   LOS ANGELES

To

my son-in-law

ROBERT GORDON HUGHES

who, before his untimely death,
singularly exemplified in his splendid
Christian character and effective Christian service
the principles of Christian action
herein stated

CONTENTS

For I long to see you, that I may impart unto you some spiritual gift, to the end ye may be established.

—Romans 1:11

But the God of all grace, who hath called us unto his eternal glory by Christ Jesus, after that ye have suffered a while, make you perfect, stablish, strengthen, settle you.

—1 Peter 5:10

FOREWORD

FEW LEADERS in American Protestantism are better qualified to discuss authoritatively the particular phase of evangelism covered in this book than is Dr. Arthur C. Archibald. He has had a long and distinguished ministry in several of our largest churches, both in the United States and in Canada. The churches which he has served have been marked by very large gains in membership. But he has put the major emphasis in fashioning his converts into efficient churchmen and churchwomen.

This volume is the logical sequel to his earlier book, *New Testament Evangelism*, published in 1946, and so widely read across our country. Taken together these two books set forth the author's creative approach to this question of such vital concern to the Christian churches. On every side it is recognized that one of the major weaknesses of modern Protestantism is at the point of conserving and integrating its converts. Dr. Archibald is not content to allow Protestantism to neglect this vital matter longer. "Evangelism," he says, "is not enough. We have become so enamored of numbers that we have lost sight of responsibility for convert development."

I confidently believe that this book will aid immeasurably in this cause of spiritual renewal.

DORES ROBINSON SHARPE

Cleveland, Ohio
February 1, 1952

INTRODUCTION

FOLLOWING the publication of my book, *New Testament Evangelism*, the publishers, feeling that the total situation had not been covered in that discussion which dealt only with evangelism, requested me to provide a manuscript on the general subject of conserving the converts. This implied the recognition of a distressing situation well known to leaders of every branch of the church; namely, that the churches are being weakened by their losses at a rate that is undermining the significance of their gains. If one can make any contribution toward remedying this situation, there is justification for attempting such a book as this.

Dr. John A. Broadus, in his able commentary on the Gospel of Matthew, wrote as follows: "Much of the work of discipling has not included that of teaching; and much of the work of teaching has ignored that of discipling." It is clear that without any relaxing in our work of making disciples, we must increase our zeal in teaching them. And the second half of the Great Commission is far more difficult than the first!

It is rather remarkable that so alarming a situation has produced so meager a literature. The writer has been unable to discover a single volume dealing specifically and adequately with this subject. Although there are a number of tracts and mimeographed articles which are excellent, it is evident that the matter has not received the serious attention that it deserves. One may hope, therefore, that the suggestions offered in this volume which is devoted entirely to this subject, may meet a felt need and assist our pastors and church leaders, who are so gravely concerned.

What I have set down here I have tried to practice in the years of a ministry that has made evangelism central, but which also has made Christian education fundamental. At the close of each year it has been my habit, with the list of our church accessions of the previous twelve months before me, to ask: "Where are these converts? What has happened to them? How far has each of them been definitely integrated into the life of the church and into the program of the Kingdom?" I have come to regard the answers I can make to these questions as the major test of the effectiveness of my ministry. Names enrolled upon church books do not, in themselves, have great significance. How far have we advanced these new members in the achievement of Christian character? How far have we succeeded in making genuine churchmen out of our converts?

The writer is deeply conscious of his limitations and failures in this matter. But also he has been thrilled to see hundreds of converts in the process of developing mature Christian personalities; he has rejoiced to see them become useful church members. What he has learned, he gladly shares.

ARTHUR C. ARCHIBALD

Cleveland, Ohio
January 15, 1952

1

THE HOLE IN THE SACK

EVANGELISM, as traditionally defined, is not enough. In most of our churches the door is opened every Sunday for the reception of new members. The door we have in mind is the front door. Our fatal blunder is that, while opening the front door on Sundays, we leave the back door open for the balance of the week. On one day the new members walk in; on six days they walk out. How can that procession out the rear door be stopped? No more timely advice can be given to our churches than this, "Close your back doors."

The results of our evangelistic efforts are largely being lost through this alarming march back into the world. If some method can be devised for holding and developing the hundreds and thousands of people we win to a profession of faith, we shall bring a new day of glory to the kingdom of God. A study of the statistics from all major denominations for the past twenty years reveals that nearly 40 per cent of our evangelistic recruits are lost to the church within seven years of their reception.

It is admitted everywhere that this business of retaining our converts, of developing them and enlisting them in great Kingdom projects, represents the weakest and most vulnerable line in present-day Protestant strategy.

One must not discount, even by suggestion, the importance of recruiting new members for Christ and His church. But we have signally lacked the same measure of fervency in nurturing the converts into full discipleship. The statistics supplied by one of our larger denominations, one which has recently made a very special effort in evangelism, are startling. Twenty years ago the membership of that body stood at 1,419,833. Today its membership stands at 1,541,991. Nearly the same as twenty years ago. Yet in that period there were 1,080,062 additions. In other words, that body lost its members almost as fast as it gained them. While many, of course, were removed by death, those who died represent only a small percentage of the total loss. In general, we lose each year approximately one-third as many members as we welcome on profession of faith. That is our real problem.

The figures of two other great church bodies which we have investigated are in line with those just stated. One of them, twenty-two years ago, had a membership of 4,499,608. Two years ago its membership stood at 4,622,444. In those twenty years it had welcomed 4,122,354 new members. By a conservative estimate, nearly one-quarter of those new members were no longer active in the life of that denomination. The other body, with a membership twenty years ago of 1,233,455, today has a membership of 1,766,678. In that period it had welcomed 1,103,346 new members. Its percentage of retentions, however, was higher. It is enlightening to discover that this denomination, more than most other bodies, puts emphasis upon education and missions.

In no part of the world is the work of evangelism pressed more energetically than in the United States. A new tide of interest is now surging through our evangelical bodies. "Crusades" galore appear upon the horizon of our church life. Yet, in spite of all such efforts in the winning of new converts, the number of "lost" church members multiplies steadily. We had our chance with those people. They were sufficiently interested at one time to come into church membership. For a brief period they were a part of the Christian fellowship. Then we began to miss them. Finally, after they had been carried on the rolls for a number of years and had not been heard from, their names were "dropped."

In all our churches, at nearly every official board meeting, someone asks about the "dead timber" being carried. Thousands today are on the verge of having their names erased. Nor can we measure our losses merely in terms of those we are inclined to "cut off." What of the vast throng in our church membership who have no vital interest, who show no devotion or conse-cration, and who are held merely by the chains of duty and respectability? They constitute another aspect of this tragic situation within modern Protestantism. We are failing to conserve and develop our committed members.

Evangelism, we repeat, is not enough. We have be-come so enamored of numbers that we have lost sight of our responsibility for training the converts whom we have received into our fellowship. God's apparent hesi-tancy in sending upon us a great spiritual awakening may be due in part to the utterly ineffective job He sees we have done with those He already has given to us.

Of course, it is easy to draw unjustified conclusions from the figures cited. We hear critics among both clergy and laity say: "Let us stop seeking so many converts; what God wants is quality, not quantity." At a meeting recently a young minister declared: "I am not interested in evangelism. I have more than enough work in taking care of what I have." Some seek in this fashion to justify their dearth of evangelistic passion and the absence of a spirit of outreach in their churches. Such persons are working under a false premise. They seem to think that evangelism and conservation are mutually exclusive. But God does not put quality over against quantity. He wants both, and He expects both. The churches can have both. If we minimize either, we are indeed guilty before God.

Just as God and man both have part in securing the convert's committal, so it is also in the matter of the convert's conservation and development. Indeed, it seems that here the human element is even more pronounced; that God places even greater responsibility upon His people. Dr. Roland Q. Leavell, in his book *The Romance of Evangelism*, gives these startling statistics concerning the status of those uniting with our churches:

20 per cent never pray.
25 per cent never read their Bible.
30 per cent never attend church.
40 per cent never give to any cause.
50 per cent never go to Sunday school.
60 per cent never attend Sunday evening service.
70 per cent never give to missions.
80 per cent never go to prayer meeting.
90 per cent never have family worship.
95 per cent never win a soul to Christ.[1]

Why? That is one of evangelism's most serious problems. Most of our churches are like a fisherman who puts his fish into a sack with a hole in the bottom. These delinquent church members are not necessarily hypocrites.

[1] From *The Romance of Evangelism*, by Roland Q. Leavell. Copyright, 1942, Fleming H. Revell Company. Used by permission.

Some, of course, were never really converted. Most of them, however, were genuinely sincere in their profession of faith. But too often we forget that they are only "babes in Christ" (1 Cor. 3:1). Babies need tender care and nurture. For want of it, the infant mortality rate among the spiritual babes in our churches is tragically high.

A statement attributed to President James A. Garfield brings us close to the heart of education. In an address before the alumni of Williams College, he is reported to have paid tribute to Mark Hopkins, the honored president of that institution, in these words: "My definition of a university is Mark Hopkins at one end of a log and a student at the other." Mark Hopkins' distinguishing gift as a philosopher and teacher was not in the information he was able to impart; it was in his ability to stimulate the thinking of his students. Is there not a suggestion here respecting the ministry? An ideal ministry not merely wins men; it also develops them in Christian character. It enlists them in Christian service.

We may well ponder the words of Ezekiel 34:2-4: "Son of man, prophesy against the shepherds of Israel, prophesy, and say unto them, Thus saith the Lord God unto the shepherds; Woe be to the shepherds of Israel that do feed themselves! should not the shepherds feed the flocks? . . . but ye feed not the flock. The diseased have ye not strengthened, neither have ye healed that which was sick, neither have ye bound up that which was broken, neither have ye brought again that which was driven away, neither have ye sought that which was lost." "He that winneth souls is wise" (Prov. 11:30) ; but we are more than heralds of good tidings. As ministers we are pastors, teachers with responsibilities of oversight, development, and training. The question is not simply, "Did you get your man?" Equally important is, "Did you keep your man?"

I went several years ago to a Midwestern city to serve as pastor. After a few months the church was faced with a building proposition of an unusually challenging character. A matter of half a million dollars was involved. I discovered that I had a church composed of "hilarious" givers (literal rendering of 2 Cor. 9:7). No sacrifice was too demanding for them to make. The money came freely, amazingly, and the great task was soon completed. When I studied their unusual spirit of giving, I soon discovered the cause. Twenty years before, that church had had a pastor who had been a magnificent teacher. He had taught every convert, and his older members as well, the meaning, methods, and benefits of Christian stewardship. They had accepted his teaching, and now as mature Christians they were openhearted and enthusiastic about the Lord's work. That minister had conserved his converts through stewardship education.

The situation today, most emphatically, is serious. We have received many converts. But in ten years, will our churches be any stronger? Will these converts be men and women of Christian stature? Will they be enlisted in Kingdom tasks? Or will they, like so many of their predecessors, have left us and gone back to "the weak and beggarly elements" of this world (Gal. 4:9)? Can we establish our converts in Christian character? Can we conserve them for our church organizations? For Christian service? For Kingdom action? Can we close the hole in the bottom of the sack? That is a matter of immediate and transcendent importance.

2

WHO IS AT FAULT?

OCCASIONALLY one is shocked by the attitude of older church members toward new converts. I have been in meetings of church boards when one of the new members happened to be the topic of conversation. One might suppose from the remarks that the function of the board was to dissect the new recruit. His failings, his remissness in duty, his lack of responsiveness to church programs, his failure to become enthusiastic over church projects, his persistence in certain petty habits—all these were tossed from man to man with supercilious judgment and a sense of superior attainment. "I never thought he would make good." "It is exactly what I expected." "After all, his background begins to tell; he shows the family weakness." And so, on and on. It seems never to occur to these critics of the failing convert that the fault may be, in part, their own; and that in most cases it is not—definitely not—so much the unfaithful convert as the unfaithful church that should be called to judgment.

If the convert is a "babe in Christ," as Paul implies, one of the indisputable demands of life is that the "babe" shall be nurtured—planned for, cared for, sacrificed for. Such adjustments must be made in the home life as will make possible the "babe's" healthy development and

19

character growth. Yet in a vast number of our churches no such responsibility is felt; instead, there is a feeling that now that the convert is in the church, the task is finished. "Do we not provide Sunday schools, youth societies, recreational facilities, and extrachurch activities such as the Y.M.C.A.—all aimed at the development of the youth?" All of these are good, up to a certain point; yet, realistically, we must admit that as a means of satisfactory soul culture such agencies have proved woefully inadequate.

The responsibility of the church for the nurturing of the converts grows out of the fact that they have voluntarily committed their lives to the church for development and Christian culture. They believe in the church and upon entering it are enthusiastic and idealistic. They look to the church as their foster mother. At this point the church, particularly in dealing with young converts, makes some tragic blunders. One of these lies in the absurd attempt to produce in the life of youth an adult experience. Throughout history, to a large degree, children and young people have been swept into the church, or out of it, as inevitable attachments to their parents; they reflect their parents' moods, minds, and practices. From the earliest days, when the new Christian movement grappled with Greek philosophy and so laid the foundation of its theology, the church has addressed itself largely to the thinking and acting of mature men and women. All too frequently it has put its dependence upon the power of the gospel to move, change, and direct the powers of mature life.

It is now generally agreed that the rise of the Sunday school movement in 1780 marked a turning point in the history of the church. Yet it is a well-known fact that Robert Raikes and his movement were regarded by his

contemporaries as a threat against the official church
leaders of his day. Robert Raikes was a Christian, but
he did not establish his first school in a church building
or as an officially recognized part of a church program.
He went outside the church to meet a human need. Many
movements that minister to vital Christian culture have
had to grow up outside the church, because the church
at first failed to show any concern. For example, the
Y.M.C.A. was founded by a churchman who saw outside
the church an opportunity for service which the church
did not provide. Only with the passing of time, have
these movements been understood and incorporated
within the Christian program. Historically, one is forced
to the conclusion that the failure in convert culture has
been due primarily to the church, not to the convert.

Local churches differ widely with respect to convert
culture. In a ministers' meeting in Boston, one of the
pastors declared that he did not believe in evangelistic
meetings. He gave, as a reason, that whereas he had received one hundred and five new members through the
work of an evangelist, only twenty of them were still in
active affiliation with his church after two years. There-
upon another pastor said: "That is very strange, for
I welcomed one hundred and twenty members under the
ministry of that same evangelist, and on looking over my
church roll recently I was gratified to discover that all
but six of that group are consistent-living members of
my church." Why this difference? One church safe-
guarded and trained the converts; the other stopped with
evangelism and accepted no responsibility for the Christian nurture of the converts.

The real opportunity of the church begins at this point.
The evangelistic effort may be ever so thorough, but if
the work of convert culture is not equally thorough, a

very large proportion of what has been gained will be lost. If the results of the numerous evangelistic campaigns are to be conserved for the kingdom of God, the churches must nurture, guide, and direct the converts as they have never done before.

Following a fruitful evangelistic campaign, a church official was heard to remark: "Just wait and see; most of the converts will not hold out." Such a declaration is little short of criminal. The spirit that prompts it never gives one word of encouragement or counsel to those who are earnestly trying to follow Christ. It is the great business of every church so to order its life that its converts will become worthy churchmen. To fail to do so is to betray them. It cannot truthfully be denied that often the churches have been more interested in getting names on their rolls than in caring adequately for those already recruited. In Old Testament times, God rebuked Israel for her pride in numbers. Today, when this larger conception of life-development is fully recognized, the matter of adding names to a church roll will be seen to be merely the first step in a lifelong journey.

If the convert is to maintain himself spiritually, he must find a warm fellowship within the church. To deny to our converts a genuinely cordial welcome is to doom these "babes in Christ" to spiritual immaturity. The manner in which some of our churches welcome their new members is shameful. They receive them with an indifference that seems to bespeak a lack of confidence in them. Our bearing seems to say: "Well, we hope you are converted, but we doubt it. We trust you will do better than the common run of young Christians, but we do not expect it. Do the best you can, and if you fall by the wayside we shall drop your names and be through with you." Happily, this is not true of all of our churches.

"We then that are strong ought to bear the infirmities of the weak, and not to please ourselves. . . . Wherefore receive ye one another, as Christ also received us to the glory of God" (Rom. 15:1, 7). Yes, there is the unfaithful church as well as the unfaithful convert.

Frequently the evangelist or the pastor is censured because of the failure of the new members to persevere in the Christian life, when in reality the failure is due to the indifference and neglect of those into whose fellowship they have come. We shall have more to say on this subject later. Dr. John A. Broadus used to tell how he once asked a Negro why it was that oxen always walked so slowly. The reply was: "I don't know, boss, cep'n dat dey always break in de young oxen wid de old ones. De old ones walk slow and dey teach de young ones to walk slow." If our young converts fade out into flavorless, negative, indifferent religionists, it is more than likely because the older church members have taught them so to do. Enthusiasm is contagious. If the church members have it, the young converts are sure to catch it. Too often they come among us with burning fervor, but by our coldness we discourage them.

Any large influx of new converts necessitates numerous changes and adjustments in church procedure. One occasionally finds a church where the older members are fiercely jealous of their prerogatives, and where they demand that the church facilities and organizations be kept wholly in their hands. Yet when a convert enters our fellowship he should find a curriculum of activities and opportunities for service made ready for his coming. This will call for a modified and enlarged church program. The educational, service, and recreational activities offered, should be so planned as to contribute to his growth in Christian conviction and to the fixing of Christian habits in his new life. This may require the setting up of new organizations, such as youth councils, youth publications, recreational functions, evangelistic outlets, community tasks, and diversified types of classroom work. How far is the program of the average church deliberately planned to provide for the development of its converts?

The Great Commission includes so much that it is not surprising that some parts of it should receive insufficient emphasis. It is surprising, however, that we should have overlooked so important a section as "teaching them to observe all things whatsoever I have commanded you" (Matt. 28:20). That is really the climax of this Christian charter. The Great Commission is a command for both evangelism and conservation.

Note that it is not a matter of teaching merely the commands of Christ; it is a matter of teaching the *observance* of those commands. Those who evangelize and baptize men must teach them the full responsibility of obeying Christ in all things—and then *show them how to do it*. Much of the work of discipling has not included this work of teaching; and much of our teaching has not included discipling. We need a better balancing of these two supreme functions. We must not relax our zeal in making converts; we must redouble our efforts in "teaching them." To fail to do this is to betray those committed to our care.

This last requirement of the Great Commission is far more exacting than the first requirement. It demands more patience, skill, preparation, and persistence of effort. That is probably why we are so inefficient at it. This work of teaching does not appeal to some because they cannot tabulate results. But what an important and glorious task it is! To make genuine Kingdom leaders out of our immature converts! To break down stubborn prejudices, to eradicate materialistic values, to implant a sense of inner, spiritual motivation, to cultivate decisiveness and strength of will with respect to the clear teachings of Christ!

This is the challenging task given to the church. Jesus spent the major portion of His ministry in doing these things. Convert culture may be said to have consumed the major portion of His time. Did it pay? The answer is in His twelve men who changed the world.

CHAPTER

3

CONSERVED TO WHAT?

IN A large gathering where the conservation of converts was being discussed, one participant struck a jarring note by saying: "I have listened with interest, and I hope with profit, to this discussion. It seems to me that most of you are discussing conservation without first asking, 'To what should the converts be conserved?' " He had asked a searching question.

What do we mean by "conserved"? Many seem to feel that a convert has been conserved if he is faithful to his church, attends it regularly, and supports it financially. We have known many converts who met this threefold test, but of whose real conservation to the inner meaning of the Christian gospel we are, to say the least, doubtful. Perhaps the term "conservation" is not the best. As popularly understood, it may suggest a negative or passive attitude. The word "development" may be superior. At least, "development" suggests growth, movement, advance. A dead object, a curio of yesterday, may be conserved, but not developed. And the convert is a living individual.

True conservation consists in the deepening and enlarging of those Christian attitudes of faith, reverence, surrender, love, obedience, co-operation, and service, which are born within the soul in that holy moment of conversion when the convert first says: "Here I am; I yield myself utterly to Thee. Henceforth I am to be with Thee and for Thee, through time and eternity, to assist Thee in securing the objectives Thou art seeking for mankind." These attitudes must not to be permitted to perish. If they are recognized and fostered through such agencies as a true church devises, they ultimately will blossom out and be strengthened until the convert reveals in all his conduct the beautiful characteristics of a true child of God.

One of the great convictions that should ever master us is that these reborn souls can grow. They come among us demanding as their heritage the right to grow. What a span between that little Scotch baby boy, born in a humble, poverty-stricken home, and the great emancipator of Africa, David Livingstone! What a journey from that underprivileged girl of Aberdeen to Mary Slessor, the flaming angel of Africa!

No task makes larger demands upon Christian leadership than inspiring and guiding a growing soul. The moment we sincerely desire to develop in the soul of children, youth, or adults that reverence for life, that constant and all-inclusive good will, that heroic consecration to the building of a new day called the kingdom of God, we quickly discover how unworthy and inept we are.

> "Lord, who am I to teach the way
> To little children day by day,
> So prone myself to go astray?
>
> "I teach them *knowledge*, but I know
> How faint they flicker and how low
> The candles of my knowledge glow.
>
> "I teach them *power* to will and do,
> But only now to learn anew
> My own great weakness through and through.

"I teach them *love* for all mankind
And all God's creatures, but I find
My love comes lagging far behind.

"Lord, if their guide I still must be,
Oh let the little children see
The teacher leaning hard on Thee."[1]

After the new birth comes the new life. A moment is enough for life's beginning, but the growing of a soul should be the holy, happy business of a lifetime. A strong and noble life is the result of orderly and cumulative processes. It is "first the blade, then the ear, after that the full corn in the ear" (Mark 4:28). We are to be conservers of life, but to what, then, is life to be conserved?

We must conserve our converts to *the possibility of growth*. The determining factor in all our thinking about these converts whom we receive into our church fellowship must be this: that their first decision is not the ultimate goal of life; it must be followed by years of growth. Their first decision is not so much something to which they look back, as it is a point of departure into a new life of fellowship and development in Christ. Perhaps this is the ultimate test of the genuineness of one's initial experience. "And Jesus increased in wisdom and stature, and in favour with God and man" (Luke 2:52). Yes, the Christian life is a process of daily growth. It includes growing more familiar with the mind of Christ; growing more co-operative with the will of Christ; growing into an ever-increasing willingness to be sent into any type of service when He calls; growing more humble, more loving, more helpful, more unselfish in all one's relationships.

[1] "The Teacher," by Leslie Pinckney Hill. Copyright by the author. Used by permission.

This process of growing is not confined to the child convert. It is probably true that the period that most frequently either makes or breaks human beings is the period of transition from childhood to adulthood. The youthful convert stands at the crossroads. Modern educators now insist that childhood is not always the most significant time for learning. They say that the process of learning is lifelong.

The churches have been held too long by the fallacy that the instruction which they give to little children in their Sunday schools will carry them in the way they should go until life ends. When the churches provide religious instruction only for children, they tacitly admit that their expectancy for spiritual growth does not go beyond childhood. But this theory as to the effectiveness and permanence of childhood conditioning is itself subject to keen scrutiny. The church can no longer regard childhood education as sufficient, for the ability to learn does not terminate with youth. Learning continues wherever problems are met and must be solved.

Furthermore, ideals of righteousness cannot be accepted as a finality once and for all. They must grow, become higher and more real, with the passing of time; otherwise our race will perish. Wordsworth, with keen perception, wrote:

> "The Youth, who daily farther from the east
> Must travel, still is Nature's priest,
>   And by the vision splendid
>   Is on his way attended;
> At length the Man perceives it die away,
> And fade into the light of common day."

But that must not happen. All is lost, if the "vision splendid" is allowed to "die away, and fade into the light of common day." Yet that is precisely what occurs all too often. A deadly fatalism creeps upon us and we say to ourselves: "Life is not worth the struggle; we are what we are and that we shall be to the end." But God says differently. We are to keep on growing in faith, power, joy, love, achievement, till the night ends and the day breaks.

Our converts are to be conserved to *Christian character*. People with dynamic and growing Christian personalities are probably the greatest single need of our modern world. The heavy burdens of a progressive social order are never going to be carried by men of famished and emaciated character. The great enterprises of the kingdom of God will never be initiated or promoted by men and women of undernourished spiritual life. The story of the church's heroes and saints is the story of leaders who, whatever their physical limitations may have been, were in spirit robust and vigorous Christians.

The Christian church is, or should be, more interested in the production of Christian character than in any other thing. Its creeds, confessions, dogmas, organizations, and activities, all exist for that purpose. It offers salvation *from* something; namely, from those things that destroy character; and it offers salvation *to* something; namely, to the abundance of life and the richness of character to be found in Jesus Christ. The chief task of the church, then, is to produce Christian personalities. Its program must be built around that purpose. We are campaigning to enlist souls in the long process of developing a special type of personality called "Christian." The entire Christian cause will be judged by our failure or our success in attaining that objective.

This means that the task of the church is not merely evangelism, as too often narrowly conceived, but also the nurture, education, development, and guidance of the committed life until there is achieved a stabilized Christian manhood or womanhood. Every activity of the church, whether educational, musical, or recreational, has this objective—the building of Christian personality. In conversion there is a change in one's inner attitudes, the beginning of a new life. That change makes growth and achievement possible. God and man then unite in the glorious task of creating that masterpiece of creation, a Christian character.

We understand, therefore, that evangelism and Christian education are really parts of the one process. Evangelism pertains to its beginnings; Christian education to its completion. There can be no worth-while evangelism apart from Christian education; and there can be no genuine Christian education apart from evangelism. The evangelist and the educator are working at the same task and are indispensable to each other. The final test of evangelism is its ability so to change life attitudes that the process of Christian education will be welcomed and entered upon; the final test of Christian education is its ability to produce Christian personality.

It is not so much what the teacher gets John and Mary to *know*, or what he gets them to *do*, as what he helps them to *become* in their total personalities. Mere acquisition of Bible facts and the memorization of Bible verses will not of themselves keep children out of the juvenile courts, but the assimilation of biblical principles of truth and conduct will be mightily constructive.

Nor does mere service, unrelated to Christian truths, guarantee a change in personality. Activity may be largely meaningless. For example, stunt singing, even when heartily engaged in, may be only a cheap substitute for worship. When a pastor stated that he expected two thousand at his Sunday school next Sunday, he was asked by one present what he expected to do with them. "Oh, we'll stuff them in somewhere," he replied. But there is not much virtue in merely getting people to make a trip to a church building, if it ends there. The supreme product of the church is a Christian personality, ever pressing toward perfection.

Furthermore, we must conserve our converts in order that they may become partners in *the redemptive task of God.* They must be enlisted as courageous champions of the full Christian gospel as applied to every phase of human life. Thousands of our recruits have left us in recent years because the conception of the Christian life we offered them was too small, too narrow and constricted, to hold their interest. Only a great task can hold great men to a great discipleship. Men will not remain loyal to an institution or a life unless they see in it some meaning or purpose of sufficient greatness to challenge their souls.

It follows, therefore, that we must have a faith and a task which, by their essential significance, will dignify the average life. Somehow we must instill in our converts the conviction that they are now a vital part of a redemptive society, in which resides the one hope for human happiness, indeed, the one hope for continued human existence. Too often our converts fail to sense the bigness of their new relationship, but converts who consciously become partners in the redemptive task of God attain to a new dignity of personal life that lifts them out of mediocrity. Few things can be more devitalizing to the average church member than the lack of a sense of vocation. He must not be allowed to feel that he belongs to an organization where he does not count. As Elton Trueblood has said, "Once a church was a brave and revolutionary fellowship, changing the course of history

by the introduction of discordant ideas; today it is a
place where people go and sit on comfortable benches,
waiting patiently until time to go home to their Sunday
dinners."[1]

Converts, however, who gain the nobler conception of
life, who come to realize that they are partners in the
redemptive task of God, have a sense of being lifted out
of mediocrity. Dr. Trueblood forcefully adds, "The basic
defect of the Protestant churches lies not in their divided
condition but in their *insipidity*."[2] This insipidity is the
product of a faith that lacks the element of adventure.
Our converts can be conserved only by channeling their
faith into challenging action. We shall escape boredom
by recovering the lost urgency of the Christian faith.
The church that evades issues, that refuses to set out
upon new and adventurous ways, cannot long hold virile
disciples within its ranks. Our converts must be conserved, therefore, by dignifying their new life, and by
patiently teaching them that they are members of a vast
redemptive society, that they have a stake and a responsibility in every community interest.

We conserve our converts only as we guide them toward
and fit them into big tasks. They must be made to feel
that, having become followers of Christ and a part of
His church, they are lifted straightway into a new significance as members of the human family. In a word,
they must be conserved not alone to the church, but to
that universal and all encompassing realm called the
Kingdom.

We need to remember, in this connection, that there
are two entities, the human soul and the human society,

[1] From *Alternative to Futility*, by Elton Trueblood. Copyright, Harper &
Brothers, 1948. Used by permission.
[2] Ibid.

and that Jesus came to save both. As Dr. D. R. Sharpe, in his book *The Call to Christian Action*, says so well: "In the men and movements of tomorrow there will be a part for you, for you are the makers of tomorrow. You are at one with the prophets . . . one with the educators, the philosophers, the poets, the dreamers, and the social engineers. . . . You are the bridge between yesterday and tomorrow. You are tomorrow's faith, courage, and love. You are the open door from a world of despair to one of promise and hope."[3] If we build our converts after this larger pattern, they will be conserved. They will become part of the task force which God has sent forth for the redemption of both the individual and society.

[3] From *The Call to Christian Action*, by D. R. Sharpe. Copyright, Harper & Brothers, 1949. Used by permission.

CHAPTER

4

THE CONVERT COMES EXPECTING

WHETHER he be a child or an adult, the convert, having passed through the exhilarating experience of confessing Jesus Christ as Lord, looks expectantly to the church of which he has become a part. It is traditional that the church expects great things of the convert, and when at times he fails to measure up, the church has not been slow in expressing its disapproval. The church unquestionably is justified in its expectations; but what the church too often forgets is that the convert, coming into it with all the thrill and joy of a new and revolutionary experience, undeniably has the right to expect certain specific things of it.

The convert has a right to expect that his church will have *faith in his sincerity.* He wants the church to believe in the genuineness of his Christian experience and to treat him as a real member of the family of God. Too often our church leaders—and older members, too, we fear—are actuated by feelings of misgiving as to the staying qualities of the new member of the flock. The convert is welcomed into an atmosphere of doubt, criticism, and probation, rather than into an atmosphere of expectation, confidence, and assurance. The new recruit sometimes is kept out of active participation in committee and organizational work for several years. The older

members insist that he must stand the test of time before
sharing in the responsibilities and activities of the church.
Thousands of converts, entering the church with fer-
vent expectation and warmth of spirit, have been so
chilled by this atmosphere of cold analysis and probation that in a few weeks they have lost all interest.
Fortunately, this attitude is not universal; but we have
seen many sad instances of it. The new convert wants
his church to have faith in him and in his Christian
experience.

The convert has a right to expect that his church, before he assumes the full responsibilities of membership,
will give him *adequate instruction*. The ignorance of the
average nonchurch person on essential Christian truths
is lamentable and alarming. Such ignorance undoubtedly
is a great menace to the moral security of America. In
a day when secular education has become almost universal, we have permitted Christian education to lag
woefully. The result is that thousands who seek membership in our churches are ignorant concerning the central
doctrines and demands of the Christian faith. They have
a right to demand that the church, before receiving them,
provide them with adequate courses of instruction, in
order that they may assume their proper place in the
church, free from embarrassment and on the basis of
intelligent co-operation in all church tasks. Pastor's
classes for converts of all ages should have a fixed place
in the program of every church. These classes will be
in addition to the greatly improved church school curriculum now being furnished by all major denominations.

The convert has a right to expect that his church will
offer him adequate opportunity for the *development of
Christian character*. The "right hand of fellowship" or
the "reception service" should never be thought of as an

attained end, but rather as the first step in a long program of Christian development. More and more we
are coming to realize that our converts are entitled to,
and look to us for, long-term training in the attainment
of Christian personality. It would be a wholesome thing
if every pastor and every church would pause to ask:
"If God should give us one hundred converts this coming
year, what would we do *with* them and what could we do
for them?" It is feared that our first thought has been
concentrated too largely on merely getting them enrolled.
We need more than evangelism, for these folk who come
to us as a fruit of our evangelistic efforts make certain
justifiable demands upon us.

Our converts have a right to demand a program of
Christian education *adjusted to their special needs*. While
our church school curriculum, as a whole, is excellent,
it is possible that more might be done in the way of
providing lessons arranged primarily for the instruction, training, and development of the converts immediately following their entrance upon church membership.
One cannot but reflect upon how helpful it would be if
every church, following the Easter period, were to offer
courses of instruction—standardized courses—in Christian doctrine, church organization and program, missionary information, the essential qualities in Christian
character, the victories of Christianity, the significance
of the church in modern life, and kindred subjects. The
converts thereby would become conversant with the
nature, scope, and significance of their new affiliation.

The convert has a right to expect that his church will
introduce him to the *great and inspiring heroes of the
faith*. Courses of study with such an objective should
be provided. The world out of which our converts come
has had little acquaintance with, and still less interest in,

the great characters the church has produced. To become strong and stable, one must live in the company of the strong and stable. To know great Christian souls, through reading their inspiring biographies, hearing them speak, meeting them personally, or sharing in their work through our gifts, is to be lifted above small, mean, and selfish things.

Our converts cannot think, live, and pray nobly, unless they walk in the company of men and women "in whose heart are the highways to Zion" (Ps. 84:5, A.S.V.). The church will bring into her program, therefore, as frequently as possible, heroes of the faith at home or abroad — missionaries and church leaders who have wrought valiantly for God. The church, furthermore, will do what it has sometimes failed to do; namely, present these outstanding people to the young who are just entering upon the Christian way of life, as well as to the adults.

One young convert, now grown to manhood, can never forget the day when one who had endured much suffering for Christ stood before the church, and the children were asked to come forward and take his hand. That youth, from that moment, was sealed forever to the life for which that great man stood. Likewise, parents who close their homes to Christian hospitality, deny their children one of the most ennobling influences that could come into their lives. Great men and women of the Kingdom, contacting young Christians, conserve and strengthen them.

The convert has a right to expect that his church will provide him with an *atmosphere of heartening good will*. The growth of the freshly committed soul is not unlike that of a bulb planted in the earth. The bulb requires a sufficient amount of warmth and sunshine, of moisture and nurturing soil. A convert enters the Christian church under such circumstances that growth may be expected to take place. But this does not always follow. Sometimes, after several years, he seemingly is less identified with the Christian program and Kingdom interests of his day than when he started. He failed to find that true and deep fellowship which would have refreshed his soul and produced genuine growth. The fellowship which means growth is not a thing external; it is of the spirit. Some churches have it; and other churches—you feel instinctively—do not.

The only way by which character grows is through experience in living. How frequently our church life is efficient in matters of organization, finance, and program, but lacking in that which is deeper and more vital; namely, a pulsating, heart-warming fellowship! When a convert finds such a fellowship in his church, he never leaves it. Because of that fellowship, his faculties are quickened and his affections are kindled. He seeks, almost unconsciously, to measure up to the high demands of his new association. He grows through the experience of worship, through Christian education, and through participation in service. But none takes rank over fellowship.

We now are beginning to see the secret of power in those early Christian churches. We discover that those churches were, before all else, centers of heart warmth. The cold Roman world had never seen anything like it. Lonely, hungry-hearted, stricken humanity, was warmed by a life-giving flame. Our new converts have a right to expect that same warmth in the church today.

Hence, each new member must be made to feel that he sits now among friends. Organizations within the church must open their doors to him. When they do not do so, they are destroyers of the fellowship. The first few months are the crucial period of the convert's life. If he is to be established in the Christian life and find his place in the church, he must be assimilated into the total loving fellowship of the church before six months have passed.

The convert has a right to expect access to *social and recreational activities*. The church must foster his whole life. Being now saved, he is to be established in body, mind, and soul. The church must recognize his social and recreational needs and make provision for them. Our Lord does not frown upon wholesome recreation. He was interested in the games of children. He watched the little ones at play and he watches their play today. In the stress and strain of modern days the older Christian also, if he is to develop a well-rounded Christian personality, needs Christian fellowship and recreation. Our converts cannot be conserved to wholesome, fully-rounded Christian character, if we deal with but a segment of their person.

CHAPTER

5

HE WORSHIPS AND STANDS FAST

HOW SHALL THE WORK of convert culture be done? This is the crux of the matter. The spirit that keeps the task before us, however, will enable us to find a way to do it. "Necessity is the mother of invention." If we really see the need of this important work, the question as to HOW to do it becomes merely a matter of individual thought, planning, and effort.

A minister, who has made an unusual record in the matter of accessions to his church, and an even better record establishing in the faith those he has won, was asked the secret of his success. He replied, "They worship and stand fast." He then explained that every effort of his entire organization was marshaled to keep new members in constant attendance upon the worship services of his church.

Many modern psychologists believe that inherited capacities have less to do with shaping personality than do external influences and fixed habits. Personality is more an achievement than an accident of heredity. It is largely the result of certain habits which can be acquired as a result of vital experiences. Whatever the heredity may be, the convert who is fostered and taught desirable habits will develop a sounder Christian personality than one who is not so guided. We co-operate with God when we assist Christians, young or old, to find and employ effective means for building Christian habits. Christian personality, of course, is far more than a mere bundle of habits, but these habits are its insignia, and they are in themselves creative in their reaction upon the soul.

Just as early in the Christian experience as possible, therefore, creative actions should become habitual—almost automatic. Habits are the forerunners of personality and its evaluation. If proper habits are developed early in the convert's life, the chances are that he will have an unbroken and continuous Christian development. Of all the conserving habits to be fixed in the life of the convert, none is more important than that of *regular participation in public worship*.

True worship, whether public or private, includes a confession to God of one's sins and failures. Such confession releases one from the hindrances which block the pathway to growth and usefulness. Through the experience of worship come also a sense of the reality of God's companionship, a knowledge and appreciation of higher values, deeper ethical insights, assistance in the solution of life's problems, a release of spiritual energies into life, and a unification of one's personality around a central ennobling purpose. Right devotional habits are a prime necessity for the conservation of the Christian convert. Communion with God in worship is the very soul of the Christian experience.

It is idle to expect the Christian experience to be permanently preserved through a use of merely external props. Social activities, athletic interests, even service projects, are not enough in themselves to achieve the stability and endurance of the new believer. They may assist, but all true conservation is primarily from within. There must be a continuous, vital experience with God. The same God to whom the convert first yielded himself must now become an ever-increasing factor in his thinking, willing, and achieving. Of the means available for creating in the convert a deeper knowledge and experience of God, none is of greater moment than that of fixing early in his new life the habit of sharing regularly in the public worship of his church. An evangelist of a few years ago, in reviving inactive church members, made use of this motto: "Every Christian in church at least once every Sunday, unless hindered by sickness or service."

Worship is the very heart of the church's program. One must confess that from the point of view of the new convert the worship services in many of our churches are poorly planned and poorly led. If the church worship services fail to assist the new convert to achieve a real feeling of devotion to God, they have failed of their central purpose. Yet, ineffective as our worship services may be, they remain the central and primary factor in the conservation of our converts.

Samuel Johnson once said: "To be of no church is dangerous. Religion, of which the rewards are distant, and which is animated by faith and hope, will glide by degrees out of the mind, unless it be invigorated and reimpressed by external ordinances, by stated calls to worship, and by the salutary influence of example."[1]

Realizing the importance of securing the habitual attendance of young converts at the worship services of the church, various devices have been employed. The unified service, the children's church, the children's missionary organization meeting during the sermon period— these, and many similar plans, all have some features of value. But they all have in common, so it seems to me,

[1] Samuel Johnson, in his *Life of Milton.*

one serious fault; namely, they remove the children from
the sanctuary worship at some time or other, thus break-
ing the quiet and reverence of the worship hour, and
destroying the unity of the family at worship. We are
the victims of a strange hallucination—that the children
are affected on Sunday by a mysterious weakness which
makes them wholly unable to remain quiet and attentive
for a period no longer than that which they all, without
complaint, pass through regularly at the public schools.
My conviction is that any method that removes the children of junior age or older from the worship service of
the church is not good. In the long run, it defeats our
main purpose.

Having tried all these methods of compromising with
the children in this matter of worship, I found, a few
years ago, what I consider to be a far better and more
effective way. I went as a pastor to a large church in
the West, and discovered at the morning worship two
hundred and fifty children sitting with their parents.
They remained through the whole service. I was amazed.
Were not these the children of whom it had been said
so often: "Poor little things; to have to sit through Sunday school and then through a whole church service—
that is asking too much of them!" Yet there they were,
and they seemed content. A large congregation gathered
each Sunday morning, but it was the children who commanded attention. How did they come to be there? What
kept them there? Then I learned the story.

A previous pastor, the late Dr. H. H. Bingham of
Toronto, finding so many of his young converts slipping
away after a few months, and believing that a child on
being converted and baptized became thereby as much an
integral part of the church at worship as his parents,
conceived this organization—"The League of Worshiping

Children." The superintendent of the League, a devoted woman, worked in closest co-operation with the Sunday school teachers. Every child under fourteen was urged to join. The children took a pledge to attend the service every Sunday morning unless hindered by sickness or absence from the city; they agreed also to sit with their parents. They signed two copies of this enrollment committal; one they kept, the other went to the League superintendent.

Each member of the League was given a booklet containing a coupon for each Sunday of the year. At tables by the two entrances to the narthex, sat two of the superintendent's assistants, to greet the children and to receive the coupon for that morning, which the child himself deposited in the League receptacle. A large record book covering a ten-year period was kept, and each Sunday afternoon the superintendent and her assistants met and entered the record for that morning. This showed which children had been absent. Then the follow-up work began. By telephone, personal call, and by letter, inquiries were made until, by the end of the week, the cause of each absence had been ascertained. To miss three Sundays without justifiable reason was to lose one's membership in the League. How was interest maintained? By stressing the importance of public worship. This church still maintains this League, and gets its reward in the building up of a great congregation.

On one Sunday morning each autumn, the entire worship service was given over to the League. Cards of enrollment were distributed at both the Sunday school and the morning worship service. Public recognition, in the form of certificates and seals, was given to those who joined the League and to those who had attended faithfully during the year. Those who had not missed attendance for five years were given a handsome New Testament. It was my delight on my first League Sunday, to present two beautiful Bibles, each with concordance and notes, to two young men who had not missed a morning service for fifteen years. They had worshiped and stood fast. They had worshiped and grown. To my certain knowledge, no young convert who united with the church during my pastorate, who also united with the League of Worshiping Children, drifted away. Of course, the church had many other agencies which appealed to the converts and strengthened them, but the experience of worship was the great convert-conserving force in that church.

What was the nature of the worship service which could hold so large a number of children through the whole period? I, as minister, of course, had my share of responsibility. When I entered that pastorate the chairman of the Board of Deacons carefully explained to me the importance of the League of Worshiping Children and the large place which it had in the hour of worship. "We have always asked our minister," he said, "to prepare one subdivision of his sermon especially for the children. We do not want him to introduce a new line of thought, but to continue with his main sermon thought, only adjusting the material to the understanding of the children. We want them to feel that the 'big sermon' is theirs as well as their parents'." I gladly agreed, for the results of the method were before me in the large number of worshiping children.

When I came to that part of my sermon I frequently would say, "And now, children, what do *you* think of what I am saying?" Then, holding to the same subject and line of thought, I would by means of the simplest language and illustrations present to them the theme I was presenting also to their parents. Having finished that subdivision, I would without announcement slip into the regular sermon treatment. I employed that method for seven years with increasing satisfaction, to the preacher at least. Without any special study or any new line of thought, the children were given an understanding of the message of the morning. It came to be that the adults would look for that portion of my sermon as eagerly as did the children.

The children's Junior Choir always had some place in the worship service, and a children's hymn was sung. In this way, we preserved the morning worship hour in unbroken reverence and in family unity.

Converts are conserved also through establishing *proper habits of private prayer and devotions.* This may be difficult to do. With every earnest desire to assist, it is not always easy to peer into the soul of another and to discover what habits and attitudes really dwell there. Only the convert himself can truly answer whether or not he prays in the silence of his soul. It is startling how many come before the membership committees of our churches who have never been taught to pray, not even the simple prayers of childhood. All their lives they have looked down, round about, but never up.

Some of my most difficult moments have been in trying to get converts to change the direction of their interest, and to frame words of true humility and supplication. Yet the pattern for future Christian development is not set until this proper facing toward God has been secured. The seeds of all growth must sprout in the secret recesses of the soul, where they are warmed and watered by the sunshine and dews of the Divine presence. The tragedy of tragedies today is that we have so many churchmen trying to live the Christian life without the Christian dynamic. Unless we can in some way establish habits of private prayer in the lives of the thousands who unite with our churches, we shall, at best, only partially conserve them.

If the pastor is to assist the convert in establishing proper devotional habits, he must know what progress the new Christian is actually making. Even as the pastor stood close to him in the hour of his conversion, so he must remain close to him in the years of his development. I have found a program of personal interviews with the convert indispensable. For the first year following his conversion, it will be well to have an interview with him every two months. On the day of his reception into the church, a card is handed to him bearing the date of appointments with the pastor for two personal interviews. These appointments I have seldom broken.

The hour with the convert can be made a very wonderful experience. Difficulties are explored, problems are faced. The convert is asked to speak frankly concerning his progress in prayer and Bible reading, his church attendance, and his activities in church organizations. No words of criticism or condemnation are uttered. But help is offered, there is a prayer together, a little tract or an attractive bit of literature is presented. Then, after an encouraging word, we part, looking forward to the next hour of interview. Difficult to get the convert to attend? Yes, sometimes. But if he understands when uniting with the church that this is part of the procedure, he usually will comply.

The convert is presented by his church, free for the first year, copies of a devotional booklet, such as *The Secret Place*. What is more, he is instructed in how to use it. Much of our excellent literature is wasted because people are not shown how best to employ it. To grow in

Christian character, one must hold frequent communion with God. The convert who does so, seldom drifts. "He worships and stands fast."

> "Lord, what a change within us one short hour
>   Spent in Thy presence will avail to make!
>   What heavy burdens from our bosoms take;
> What parched grounds refresh, as with a shower!
> We kneel, and all around us seems to lower;
>   We rise, and all the distant and the near
>   Stands forth in sunny outline, brave and clear!
> We kneel, how weak! we rise, how full of power!
> Why, therefore, should we do ourselves this wrong,
> Or others, that we are not always strong;
> That we are ever overborne with care;
>   That we should ever weak or heartless be,
> Anxious or troubled, when with us is prayer,
>   And joy and strength and courage are with Thee?"

—RICHARD C. TRENCH

CHAPTER

6

HE UNDERSTANDS AND IS UNMOVED

IT MAY BE that one reason for the ineffectiveness of much Protestant preaching is that frequently it concerns matters about which the congregation has not been adequately instructed. Understanding is the clear road to conviction and to stability. The word "understanding" here has reference to the convert's comprehension of the Christian gospel and of the gospel's bearing on the whole of life.

Too often our candidates for church membership are welcomed upon a statement of their *confusion*, rather than upon a statement of their *conviction*. It is essential, if our convert is to become a useful church member, that he come face to face *with*, and comprehend his relationship *to*, the great facts of the Christian gospel. The superficial instruction given to the candidate for church membership often is little short of criminal.

A ministerial friend of mine told me that he happened to be present when the membership committee of a neighboring church was examining candidates for church membership. Among the questions asked were: "Who was Jesus?" "Where did He live?" "What did He do?" "What had He come to do?" "What does He offer to us?" "What do we have to do to receive what He offers?" "What change will be made in a man's daily living when he becomes a Christian and a church member?" Surely, these were not difficult or unreasonable questions. Two of the candidates did not answer a single question with any evidence of real comprehension. Yet this committee, seemingly anxious to swell the membership roll of their church at whatever cost, recommended all of the candidates for membership.

While a carefully planned program of instruction should follow church membership, the best time to ground the converts in the fundamental Christian truths is before their baptism. Although conditions are improving, it remains true that many of our churches still depend upon whatever the convert may have learned in Sunday school. In some cases, the convert may have had no instruction at all. The seriousness of this situation is now recognized by all denominational leaders, and an encouraging sign is the increased number of church membership training manuals now coming from denominational publishing houses.

A considerable part of our church losses can be accounted for by the fact that those who have fallen away were never really in the church. The baptized but non-Christian additions to our churches have become our embarrassment. The screening of church members should be performed at the entrance rather than at the exit. Our membership losses will continue as long as we are willing to receive into membership those who have an insufficient understanding of the basic facts and implications of church affiliation.

Among the agencies of proven value for church membership preparation, the *Pastor's Class* stands first. Due to the warmth and tenderness of the convert's experience, he will come so close to his pastor in this instruction period that the relationship will have a wholesome influence upon him for years to come. The pastor usually is the best equipped person in the church to teach such a class.

Many pastors have made it their practice to spend not less than twenty minutes each Sunday with their junior high girls and boys throughout the pre-Easter season. When this is done, a pastor can discuss with them, simply and clearly, the many matters a young convert needs to understand if he is to become a worthy churchman. Answers may be given to such questions as "Who is Jesus Christ?" "What is salvation, and how is it received?" "After I become a church member, what is expected of me?" "What is the church trying to do in the world?" "What is the meaning of the ordinances?" "What is a Christian steward?"

A pastor in Cleveland, Ohio, maintains a converts' class every Sunday evening throughout the year. His church has a steady stream of accessions, but all must go through that class. It is not surprising, therefore, that his ministry should be marked by significant, enduring achievements. Such a class may be held on Sunday afternoon or on a weekday afternoon or evening. It can profitably be held at the pastor's home, being enriched at times by social fellowship.

A devoted Sunday school teacher can be a most effective factor in conserving the young convert. I have made it a habit, when a child unites with the church, to approach the child's teacher with suggestions as to his or her added responsibility. There should be a new emphasis in that teacher's instruction. An increased fostering care should be exercised over that member of the class. Occasionally the child should be taken aside for questioning, to ascertain what progress he is making. Is he attending church regularly? Is he reading a passage from the Bible each

day? Is he maintaining habits of prayer? Is he participating in any form of Christian service? How is he
showing, among his school companions, that he now is a
follower of Christ? One teacher opens her class period
with this question, "Children, what did you do for Christ
this past week?" What a thought-provoking question for
all of us! When a large number of Sunday school children
have united with the church at one time, I have been
careful to get all the teachers of that group together that
I might instruct them as to their new responsibility.
Happy is the church which has a group of teachers who
are more than evangelists; who also are the guardians
and educators of the new converts!

Child converts may be classified into two groups. In the
first group are the children who have been reared in
Christian homes, and whose bent of character and habits,
as a result of their home training, already has been directed toward faith in Christ. When this is the case, the
function of the Sunday school teacher as a conserver is
largely one of co-operation with the home. The teacher
seeks a further development of a religious experience
begun under favorable circumstances.

But there is usually to be found a second group of children whose background is radically different. Their religious education has been almost totally neglected. The
facts of the Christian religion are but dimly known, if
at all. They come from homes where the Christian faith
is neither held nor practiced. These children do not see
in their home environment either Christian attitudes or
responses. The new life with Christ is to them like land-
ing on the shore of a foreign land. This type of convert
sets before the devoted teacher a sobering challenge, for
only about 30 per cent who come out of such homes remain
permanently attached to the church.

One teacher of such young converts set as her goal the expression, at some point in every class session, of at least one Christian attitude. The teacher would pray before her class and thus instill in the children's minds the conviction of the vital place communion with Christ holds in Christian experience. Another Sunday she would have a form of witnessing about experiences of the week. On yet another Sunday she would have some child tell a missionary story, or she would discuss with her class some aspect of the Christian life.

Let the teacher be certain that she does not dwell merely upon negations. She should emphasize the concrete and positive nature of the Christian experience. While the convert should understand that there are many things the Christian should not do, care must be taken to interpret Christian character and life in terms of privilege and opportunity. The Christian life should be presented constantly as a challenge to co-operation in a grand and glorious crusade. The teacher frequently should point out the diversified service which the church is rendering to mankind. She should impress deeply upon the convert's mind that joining a church means having part in the relieving of distress, suffering, and injustice throughout the world, and in the bringing of mankind into one great family of good will.

An additional emphasis is needed. If the young convert from the non-Christian home is to be conserved, the pastor, the Sunday school teacher, and the church officials must unite to win that home to Christ. Why should we suppose that we can hold that boy or girl to Christian character and growth when everything we teach in church and Sunday school is openly denied and flouted by the child's parents?

Two girls, one thirteen and the other eleven, came into

my church membership class. They gave every evidence of a sincere purpose and of a deepening spiritual experience. When I visited their home, the parents consented to the girls' baptism; but they manifested an attitude of such unconcern—even declining to be present at the baptismal service—that I went away sad at heart and greatly fearful for the future of those two fine girls. Two months after their baptism, I began to miss them from church. At our conference period they told me a sad story of their home, where every conceivable discouragement was being thrown against them. I presented their situation before my deacons, and one of them said at once, "Pastor, let us win those parents to Christ." So he and his wife took that family upon their hearts. They called; they invited the parents to accompany them to a social function outside the church; they remembered them when sickness came; they sent cards on the children's birthdays; and when the mother fell one day and suffered a broken leg, leaving no one to care for the two younger children in that family, this couple took them into their home for two weeks. Then a day came when the older girl had a part in the Sunday school Christmas festival, and the deacon and his wife invited those parents to attend with them. They sat with them. They introduced them to others. To make this happy tale brief, three months later I baptized both parents. We had conserved the girls to Christ and the church by evangelizing their parents. Again and again we have discovered that in conserving the young convert the place to begin is in the home. Most homes can be won to Christ if we can find Christian people who are sufficiently devoted to undertake the task.

The adult convert stands in almost equal need of instruction and fostering care. The amount of his religious information frequently is overestimated. Often he is no better informed than the child convert. When I baptized an eighty-year-old man, he appeared at the Sunday school the following Sunday, saying: "Put me in the Primary Department. I know little if anything about this Christian way of living." Many of our older converts could well fit in just there. If a program of instruction is necessary before church membership, it is equally indispensable through the years that follow. If we fail to get our converts into educational classes, we have missed our supreme opportunity with them.

All too many of our adult converts have identified the program of Christian living with church membership. They substitute the means of religion for the goal, and consider conversion as the arrival at the destination, rather than as the beginning of a journey. Evangelism, therefore, is not enough. We must bring the converts into our educational agencies, if they are to grow "in wisdom and stature, and in favour with God and man" (Luke 2:52). The vision of a redeemed life for both the individual and society involves the possession of Christian concepts, beliefs, attitudes, motives, and practices. These concepts are not bestowed miraculously; they are an achievement. The basic need of our day is the bringing of our converts, through patient training, into fully matured Christian character.

The convert, whether a youth or a young adult, can be brought to a better understanding and deeper experience of the Christian life through identification with some department of the educational program of his church. Properly conducted *Bible classes* have a great service to render at this point. Many are inclined to belittle the Sunday school today, but as a conserving agency it has great value. A faithful, loving, intelligent teacher, explaining Sunday after Sunday the basic truths of the kingdom of

God, builds up in the members of his class a working understanding of the fundamental Christian truths. It is the first task of the pastor, therefore, to see that every convert is identified with some department of his Sunday school.

We also highly commend the direction of the social life of the youth and young adults within the church circle through suitable clubs of various kinds. The *Young Couples' Club* has proved of value as an agency for bringing young married couples together in a fine Christian fellowship. Some young people can be interested in *discussion groups* which meet once each month, and take up the leading topics of the hour, religious, social, and political. A wise leader is needed for this sort of thing, one able to stimulate and guide the discussion. Sometimes, at the close of the discussion, a secret ballot is taken to ascertain which side, in the judgment of those present, has stated better the Christian position. Frequently, when there has been uncertainty as to the conclusions reached, the pastor has been given a ten-minute opportunity to summarize and conclude the discussion. I have had as high as one hundred and ten enrolled in one of these discussion groups. Every phase of Kingdom interests can be frankly faced to the edification of all participating.

At least once each year, the church should conduct a *School for Christian Living.* Such a school can be an effective conserving agency. When sufficiently publicized in advance, and when its purpose has been fully explained to the entire congregation, it can enroll at times nearly half the membership of the church. Such a school meets for six or seven evenings in as many weeks. Those who attend, enroll in various classes for a study of the practical application of the gospel to their immediate problems of living. A great variety of courses may be offered; such as: "Building a Christian family relationship"; "How would Christ have a family budget its income?"; "Home guidance for children"; "The foundations of successful marriage"; "The home and its community"; "The home and the public schools"; "The home and the church." Two classes of fifty minutes each, with a twenty-minute assembly period between, provide a profitable program to which young adults will look with increasing interest.

It seems scarcely necessary to emphasize the conserving power upon young converts of *summer camping* experiences conducted under Christian auspices. Back from one of these camps came three young fellows who had drifted far from the church, to say to me, "Pastor, around the campfire, as the chaplain spoke, we felt again our need of God and the church." My advice to all pastors is that they make every effort to raise the funds needed to insure the attendance of their young converts at summer camps.

The convert is conserved also when, through the *missionary organizations* of his church, he gains a sense of the world-wide significance of the Christian movement of which he has become a part. If we keep our Christianity big, we can hold the greathearted. The missionary organizations and programs of the church become thereby a mighty conserving force. The convert should join some organization of the church. Seventy-five per cent of those whom we lose never united with any church organization.

Conserved through understanding! There can be no effective conservation apart from it. If the convert, whether child, youth, or adult, is really to be built up in Christ and preserved to the church, he must be continually learning. The educational program of the church must enroll and hold the convert from childhood to the end of life's journey.

More and more we are sensing that the survival of the human race depends upon the survival of Christian character. Christian ideals must be made progressively dominant. The church is under a solemn obligation to devise and maintain educational agencies for the training of its converts. Because childhood formulas will not be adequate for adults, its program of Christian education must be so designed as to meet the needs of every period of life. The church must teach its converts how to live a soundly Christian life in an unchristian society. The converts have a right to look to the church for some system of Christian education which will guide and sustain them through all their years.

CHAPTER

7

HE FELLOWSHIPS AND IS IDENTIFIED

WHAT MINISTER is there who has not heard repeatedly the excuse from those who have fallen away: "Your church was not sociable; nobody spoke to me, and nobody cared whether I came or not"? In many cases the fault lies almost entirely with the complaining individual. There are folks so constituted that they will find no fellowship anywhere they may go. Yet it must be admitted that in many of our churches the spirit of fellowship is not all that it should be. In some churches almost the only expression of fellowship which the new convert finds is the formal handshake at the door on Sunday morning. He slips in, he slips out; who cares very much if he should be absent?

If the converts are to be conserved through fellowship, many of our churches will have to change their spirit and attitude. The "come-if-you-will" or "stay-away-if-you-will" spirit will have to go. On entering some churches one immediately feels an encompassing warmth; there are other churches so stiff, cold, and self-satisfied that one is chilled to the marrow. If we are going to conserve our converts, we shall have to kindle fires of warmth and welcome.

The convert, by reason of the nature of his experience, may be a very lonely individual. If ever a man is isolated

60

in the depths of his being, it is in that revolutionary moment when he turns to his Lord and in a complete reversal of his life-attitudes says, "Thou art my Savior and my Redeemer." But if the convert remains in isolation, he stands in grave danger. The spiritual experience of conversion should flower almost at once into fellowship. To provide such fellowship, God has created His church. Happy is the new disciple who finds in the church those of like mind and purpose who welcome him to their hearts. From that hour the convert's spiritual progress begins.

The ideal life is not attained by the solitary Christian, nor by the unattached disciple. In long-continued solitude, something dies that in the busy stream of life would have put on strength and beauty. In the New Testament the word "saint" never designates an individual who became holy by living apart. On the contrary, the Scriptures make it clear that the human soul grows saintly in society. An intimate friend of an eminent statesman wrote in explanation of his failure: "He was the loneliest man I ever knew. His greatest fault was that he worked too much alone." A notable missionary who worked for many years in almost unendurable loneliness, and who often was depressed nearly to the point of self-destruction, wrote: "No worker should be alone; every man should have colleagues."

When the pastor or the evangelist urges his converts to unite immediately with the church, he evaluates rightly the helpful, stabilizing value of fellowship. Christian personality grows most surely and securely under warming contacts with other Christians. The religious life is best renewed and maintained by constant interaction between religiously minded people of a common faith and practice. There is much talk today of "a church outside the church." But there is only one church, and it is not outside the body of our Lord. The church is the divinely appointed home for all true followers of Christ. There, in the high fellowship of God's chosen, their souls grow and they can render a service worthy of their calling. A mature Christian character cannot be achieved in isolation.

The desire for fellowship is one of the basic longings of the soul. One wonders at the strong hold that service clubs have upon the leading men of a community. The only secret is that these organizations offer to their members a fine fellowship. Back of all their stunts, singing, backslapping, and first-name calling, men are finding that which they had lost; namely, the happy spirit of fellowship they knew as boys. If men sing together and laugh together, they come really to know one another. A familiar jingle puts it thus:

"There's nothing like the comradeship which warms the lives of those
Who make the glorious circle of the 'Jacks' and 'Jims' and 'Joes.' "

There is nothing like it, that is, except the fellowship within the church of God!

For instance, the young convert may be facing the alcohol problem. Will he drink or will he abstain? The group thinking and the group conclusions will have a significant effect upon him. He will arrive at a decision which is not his alone, but which is partly the result of the creative thought of the entire fellowship. Individual decisions are sustained and strengthened by fellowship thinking and conclusions. The new convert who never finds such a fellowship is deprived of one of the mainstays of Christian character and achievement.

In *Young People's Method in the Church,* Dr. Roy

Burkhart gives an illustration of how the Christian character and ideals of young people are developed when they find real fellowship. In a certain prominent church there was a youth group. Some of the group lived in the Hill and Dales, the wealthy part of the town; others lived in the Walnut Hill district, "across the tracks." Needless to say, there were cliques in that church. Those with money made the decisions and took the important places.

Then one day there came to that church a young man who found it in his heart to do something for the young people. Up to that time the church had given little thought to them. For three years this young man worked. He sent young people to summer camps. He persuaded the men of the church to give up their basement room that it might be used for youth recreational purposes. After a time he was able so to interpret worship that the wealthy and the poor young people worshiped together, prayed together, served together, and lived together without a consciousness of any differences on the economic level. These young people, as a group, began to evaluate society in the light of the mind and teaching of Jesus Christ.

Dr. Burkhart relates that he visited this group one Sunday during a worship hour. The leader of the service was the son of a millionaire realtor, and the pianist was a beautiful girl from the west side. A boy from the Walnut Hill district sat beside the visitor. At the close he remarked: "Things have changed around here. We have a wonderful group and a great spirit. The boy who led the services, the son of a millionaire, and the girl who played the piano are engaged. Money is incidental to this group. The ideals of Jesus are what count here."[1]

[1] From *Young People's Method in the Church*, by Hayward and Burkhart. Copyright, 1933, by The Abingdon Press, Inc. By permission of Abingdon-Cokesbury Press.

The power of fellowship control had produced this remarkable change. No member of that group, by himself, would likely have arrived at such a new Christian attitude, but together they had worked it out. John Dewey once said, "The best way to save a young man is to save his group." Without fellowship there can be no enduring growth.

Church fellowship, to be effective, must be planned and promoted. While in a very real sense it is first of all a spirit, an atmosphere, a temper, yet without careful planning, even a fine spirit of fellowship will not achieve what is desired. Conservation through fellowship should begin with the convert's first contacts with the church in which he is seeking membership. A warmhearted welcome should be extended by the membership committee.

For years I have made it a habit to have some member of the membership committee accompany each candidate when he comes before that body and is proposed for membership. This sponsor takes the candidate in charge and presents him to the various members of the committee. Each member in turn has a word of cordial greeting. The sponsor then presents the candidate to the whole committee, giving a bit of information concerning him—biographical data, experience, occupation, etc. Following the questioning period, he takes the candidate to an adjoining room where another man is waiting to have fellowship with him while the committee is acting upon the application. When a decision has been reached, the sponsor goes out and brings the candidate back and reports to him, with an expression of gratitude and joy, the favorable action of the committee. He then presents the candidate with a small, printed pamphlet containing instructions as to what further steps are to be taken in order to enter into full membership in the church. This first contact of the convert with the church should be of such a pleasant character that it will always be recalled with a sense of gratitude and deep satisfaction.

The convert's baptism and reception into the church should be made an experience so outstanding, so impressive, and so beautiful that it will never be forgotten. The average church is very careless at this point. In churches that practice immersion, the ordinance of baptism is sometimes conducted in a manner that is offensive to good taste. As a rule, the ordinance is not an integral part of the service of worship, but either precedes it or is tacked on at the close. When this is done, the ordinance lacks the dignity, beauty, and power of expression that rightfully belong to it. Instead, therefore, of making the baptismal service a mere adjunct to another service, it is well to have it at the vesper hour or in the evening, when it can be unhurried. At that time, the entire service may be given over to an explanation of the ordinance and to its administration. Equal thought should be given to the manner of observing the Lord's Supper. Care should be taken to explain its meaning to the new church member. The importance of attendance at each observance of the Lord's Supper should be emphasized.

When a special service is planned for the observance of either of these two ordinances, baptism and the Lord's Supper, there can be an appropriate arrangement of physical and ritual details, impossible when the ordinance is made a part of the Sunday morning preaching service. Musical and lighting effects can be employed to give to the observance a beauty and impressiveness which often is absent. The convert should recall his baptism and his first communion as outstanding, never-to-be-forgotten events in his life. The Roman Church makes much of the first communion. What virtue can there be in the haste and barrenness of the average celebration of the Lord's Supper in most Protestant churches?

At his first communion each new member may be presented with the following: (1) A beautifully printed certificate of baptism and church membership. This certificate may carry a picture of the church and of its pastor. (2) A pamphlet or two containing information about the local church and the denomination. (3) A pocket New Testament. (4) A stewardship pledge card for committal of time, talent, and resources. While the right hand of fellowship is being given, the sponsor of each new member stands facing the convert assigned to him or her. At the close of the service, all those in attendance may be asked to come forward and greet the new members as they stand in line. This service might well be followed by an hour of fellowship in the social hall, where light refreshments are served and where the members, new and old, have opportunity to become better acquainted. Such a service of welcome is never forgotten. It remains in years to come a mighty conserving factor.

The modern tendency in some of our churches is to belittle the spiritual effectiveness of the ordinances. But our Lord understood human nature when he set baptism and the Lord's Supper at the beginning and in the midst of the Christian experience. The Scotch churches sensed this fact aright. The profound influence of the "kirk" on the Scotch character was due in considerable measure to the importance which those churches attached to the communion service. The mailing of the "token" preceding each commemoration of the Lord's death involved both time and labor, but the effort was justified.

Sensing that conserving value, I made it a custom in

some of my pastorates to mail, during the week preceding the communion, a personal invitation card which the recipient was asked to fill in and bring to the service. These cards were collected and a careful record of attendance was kept. On the back of the invitation cards sent out each month was a report on that member's attendance for the preceding months of the year. At the close of the year there was distributed a printed list showing the communion record of all the members of the church for the preceding twelve months. This never gave offense and greatly increased attendance. It helped amazingly in integrating new members into the body of the church.

I have already mentioned the matter of sponsors. A further word may be helpful. Each new member, upon entering the church, has assigned to him by the pastor some tried and trusted older member of the church. The sponsor is publicly linked up with the convert at his first communion service. Such a sponsor will establish at once a relationship of simple, natural, warmhearted friendship. The relationship must be free from any sense of patronage; and, above all, the new member must not get the idea that he is now subject to some sort of surveillance. Before their assignment, the sponsors should be instructed by the pastor as to their duties and methods of procedure. The success of the system depends upon the effectiveness with which the sponsor can give the impression that he is sincerely desirous of being just a friend.

Only careful oversight can make this relationship really fruitful. The sponsor will take note whether the convert attends public worship with regularity. He will be alert to learn of illness or of periods of unusual stress in the convert's home. He will find out the birthday of each member of the family and give it some recognition. He will encourage the reading of denominational publications and the use of some book of daily devotions, such as *The Secret Place*. Great care should be taken in selecting sponsors. Infinite harm will be done to the converts, if they discover (as has sometimes happened) that the character and habits of those chosen to assist them are unchristian and unworthy. Where a man and wife unite with the church, the sponsors should be another man and wife.

At least twice each year the church should have a reception or other social event designed especially for those who have united with the church during the preceding six months. This should be made an outstanding event, and to it all the relatives and friends of the new members should be invited. In this way many new contacts can be made. All the fellowship resources of the church should be brought to bear on the convert very early in his new relationships. If we fail at the beginning, it is very difficult to recover lost ground. One social event of this kind during the year is not sufficient. At the annual meeting of the church, the wise pastor and officers will reserve special tables, if dinner is served, for those who have united with the church during the year. They will come as guests of the church.

One should not overlook the strong holding power of recreational programs for certain types of members. Our younger converts will find satisfaction in church fellowship through the exercise of their play instinct. Many of our church plants, although not originally constructed with this use in mind, have been modified so as to give at least limited facilities for play. Although there are still among us a few church officials who frown upon play and hold that it is not justifiable as a part of the church program, most leaders are agreed that people who have eaten together and played together develop a spirit of comradeship not always found through mere participation in public worship. Dr. Richard Hoiland well says: "Those who can have fun together can the better work together, and those who can do teamwork in play have gone a long way in learning co-operation in the work of the church."

Wholesome recreation tends to break down the force of temptation to questionable amusements and excesses. Whenever I hear someone condemning a church youth for going to the wrong places and doing the wrong things, I feel like asking: "Whose fault was it? How did it happen that this young man had to go somewhere else to satisfy his craving for play and social fellowship?" A church, if it thought it worth its while, could just as readily meet the social and athletic needs of its converts as it meets their educational and spiritual demands.

Not far from London, Ontario, there was a country parish consisting of three churches. For some time the work had been declining. On Saturday nights the youth of the district invariably drove to the city, and, too often, they returned in the early morning hours intoxicated and corrupted. The situation looked rather hopeless for those churches. Their youth had forsaken them. Then a young minister, without unusual equipment, but robust and fond of play, accepted the pastorate. After surveying the situation, he told his deacons: "We have no future here unless we stop the present trends among our youth. And we shall have to begin at the point of their interest, not of ours." The deacons promised their support. He rented an immense barn and also the field back of it. He turned the barn into a first-class gymnasium. He laid out a baseball diamond and a football field. He organized the youth on the near-by farms into teams. Every Saturday afternoon and night that barn and that field were alive with those farmers' sons at play. That minister completely reversed the habits of the young people of that district. Then he began to connect their activities with the churches. He organized youth groups for Bible study. He set in motion numerous projects for community betterment. In three years he had markedly changed the life of that community and the outlook for those three churches.

An evening devoted to recreation can often be concluded in a devotional spirit, whereby the young convert will be brought to a realization that his spiritual experience is the basis of all such fellowship. Group singing, a well-told story, a carefully chosen quartet number, a chalk talk, a brief prayer—all lend themselves to a delightful and enriching fellowship which will produce genuine growth of soul and link the new member more closely to his church.

In the case of our larger parishes, a zoning plan proves helpful. When the membership becomes very large, general fellowship in the church is somewhat difficult, and we must create fellowship on the basis of smaller units. One of our ministers, serving a church with a membership of 2,400, has his parish divided into twenty-four zones. A capable man or woman is appointed a captain over each zone. Each captain has two assistants. A list of the names and addresses of all church members in a particular zone is mailed to all the members of that zone. Once each month the members of the church who live in that zone meet together, sometimes in the church, more often in a home. An informal social time is enjoyed. Community matters pertaining to the immediate neighborhood are discussed. School problems are considered. The program of the church for the immediate future is presented. Cases of illness in the neighborhood are announced. The pastor or his assistant usually is present. There is a bit of singing and then a committee serves a light repast. This pastor testifies that 80 per cent of his people are responding to this zoning method, and that he now is losing very few of his members through lack of fellowship. New members are immediately registered in their proper zone and called upon by the zone membership.

We must in some manner impress upon our converts that in entering the Christian church they have become part of the greatest fellowship on earth. Critics of the church we have had and still have in abundance. But we are prepared to maintain against all comers that nowhere is there to be found so large and so constant a readiness for self-sacrifice, unflagging devotion, and patient fidelity to duty as in the church of Christ. For sheer moral idealism, the membership of our churches will match any group of people. Here is a world-wide fellowship, made up of all races, all ages, all languages, all occupations, all classes. Here is the largest and richest fellowship on earth, the most diversified, yet the most united, fellowship on earth. To be a member of God's universal church—what a privilege! What a joy! What a source of strength!

CHAPTER

8

HE SHARES AND IS ENRICHED

IN THE GROWTH of a Christian there are four M's which I like: "Make Membership Mean Much." It is a good motto to give to every person uniting with the church. There is much point also to the slogan, "Work for everybody and everybody at work." The pastor needs to ask himself often, "Are the new members properly placed in our church organization?"

I can never forget a bit of advice given by the late Dr. F. K. Wilson, then editor of the *Watchman*. I had invited him to speak to a class of two hundred and twenty-five converts that we were welcoming that Sunday morning into the First Baptist Church, Lowell, Mass. "My friends," he said, "my counsel to you is in three phrases. First, 'Get *in!*' Church membership is a vital necessity to you as a Christian. Second, 'Get *all* in!' Don't leave part of your life and talents belonging still to the old life out of which you have come. Third, 'Get *all the way* in!' It's a big, wide, wondrous life into which you have now come. Don't live in one little corner of it. Get into all of it through your interests, prayers, contributions, and talents." No sounder advice could have been given to those converts.

The effectiveness of a pastor and the measure of the contribution he can make to his church are to be judged, not alone by what he personally can accomplish, but also by the number of members he can effectively enlist in some form of Christian service. The pastor who trains others, when he departs, will leave behind him a strong, efficient church; but the pastor who has undertaken to do everything himself, will leave for the next pastor a group of church cripples.

Let us ask, then, these two questions: How many of our converts have we enlisted in some form of Christian service? To what extent have we taught them that the spirit of their new life is one of sharing all that they are and have with a needy humanity? This is the real test by which we, as ministers, largely stand or fall. By this test, some whose ministry seems very inconspicuous, take high rank; and some who win the applause of men take low rank in the eyes of God.

The converts uniting with our churches become strong, effective Christians to the degree that a conviction as to the stewardship of life becomes a controlling factor in their lives. That conception of church affiliation which makes of it but a pathway to heaven, a road of popular respectability, or a "thing to do because parents and friends belong," can never make robust disciples out of converts. We must somehow get the converts to understand that they have enlisted to perform a task. Having presented themselves to Christ as Lord of their lives, they are to share with all mankind whatever God has entrusted to them of time, talents, and resources. Somewhere at the beginning of their Christian experience this conviction must be born. A study of stewardship, followed by a committal to that program, will prove an important means of establishing the converts.

Every church should maintain such a class, especially for the new converts, but not for them only. The church of today is alarmingly weak in many departments of its life simply because the ideals of stewardship have never possessed the average church member. Courses in stewardship, such as have been prepared by all major denominations, follow logically upon their united efforts in evangelism. The purpose of these courses is not to secure givers of money only, but to help the new members, through a sense of belonging and sharing, to commit themselves wholly and permanently to the Christian way of living.

The convert should be enlisted promptly in some form of Christian service. Correct devotional habits are not enough. If one is to grow, one must serve. The Master said, "He that loseth his life for my sake shall find it" (Matt. 10:39). The finding of life is in the losing of it, in the expending of it; that is to say, in practical Christian service.

Unfortunately, the average church is aware of only a few places of employment for those entering its membership. If all our new members took us seriously and tithed their time in Christian service, where could they be used? As matters stand, we often are embarrassed to find a place in which a willing Christian may work. This is true in spite of the fact that we are surrounded by great areas of need. Some of these areas of need cry out for the investment of Christian time, thought, ability, and resources.

All too many of our converts are never challenged by any kind of service opportunity. Instead, the converts sometimes meet with downright discouragement. How often we have heard members of a nominating committee say: "Oh, do not use him. He is only a new member. Wait until he has had more experience"! But one can gain experience only in the doing. To deny the member a chance to serve because he is new, and for no other reason, is to deprive him of what he needs most. His happiness, strength, and stability are dependent on his participating at once in some form of Christian service.

The enlistment of new members in service activities does not come about by chance. It comes only as a result of careful planning and persistent effort. I have sometimes thought that we should have a new department in our church life, one that would correspond to a personnel or employment department. It would be composed of some of our most intelligent men and women, who constantly would be seeking out forms of Christian activity in the church and throughout the community. Such findings would be carefully filed for reference. A busy pastor cannot always keep such information ready for immediate use, but a wide-awake committee could do it. Then, when a convert united with the church the personal information sheet which he gave to the membership committee could be checked against the classified list of service openings kept on file. In two of my pastorates I employed this method with highly satisfactory results. When a person united with the church, we usually had a task ready and waiting.

To ensure the effectiveness of this system, one needs to know the particular abilities and preferences of each convert. As a suggestion as to how this may be done, I reproduce here a sample personal data sheet. This is filled in by the candidate and presented to the membership committee when he appears before that body.

NEW MEMBERS DATA FILE

In applying for membership in this church, it is my purpose not only to receive help, but also to give help, in bringing in Christ's kingdom among men. Accordingly, I have checked below the fields of service in which I think I can make my best contribution to its life and work.

DEVOTIONAL

( ) Engage in prayer for others
( ) Lead a prayer group

( ) Lead devotional meetings
( ) Distribute devotional literature

EVANGELISM

( ) Support all soul-winning efforts
( ) Be a member of an evangelistic team

( ) Will join the Evangelism Class
( ) Will do personal evangelistic visitation

EDUCATIONAL

( ) Serve as a Sunday school officer
( ) Teach in Sunday school
    Age group preferred_____
( ) Be a substitute Sunday school teacher
( ) Lead a Mission Study Class

( ) Be a Boy or Girl Scout leader
( ) Lead recreational program
( ) Be a Home Department visitor
( ) Join church training school with a view to becoming a teacher
( ) Assist in the church nursery

FINANCIAL

( ) Make a pledge to current expenses
( ) Make a pledge to missions
( ) Practice scriptural stewardship

( ) Serve on the Finance Committee
( ) Assist in the Every Member Canvass
( ) Join the Stewardship Class

MUSIC

( ) Play the piano
( ) Play in orchestra
( ) Lead orchestra
( ) Help with the music in Sunday school

( ) Sing in Junior Choir
( ) Sing in Senior Choir
( ) Lead congregational singing
( ) Soloist

DRAMATIC

( ) Direct church dramatics
( ) Participate in dramatic productions

( ) Plan programs for special days
( ) Train children for special programs

MANUAL SERVICE

( ) Fold calendars on Sunday
( ) Will wait on tables
( ) Serve in kitchen
( ) Will paint signs and posters
( ) Will assist in church office

( ) Assist in care of church property
( ) Serve as usher
( ) Operate mimeograph machine
( ) Other forms of service_____

COMMUNITY SERVICE

( ) Oppose the liquor industry
( ) Oppose gambling in every form
( ) Actively support Red Cross, etc.

( ) Will vote as a Christian
( ) Support hospitals, orphanages, etc.

The Enlistment Committee, in discovering opportunities for service and keeping the list up to date, may use such a card as this:

SERVICE OPPORTUNITY CARD

NATURE OF THE TASK?_____

CONNECTED WITH WHAT ORGANIZATION?_____

WHAT ARE THE NECESSARY QUALIFICATIONS?_____

   (1) Primary_____

   (2) Secondary_____

   (3) Age_____(4) Man or Woman_____

   (5) When is worker needed?_____

   (6) Any special conditions?_____

NAME OF NEW MEMBER ASSIGNED TO THIS TASK_____

DATE OF ASSIGNMENT_____

Ninety per cent of the latent talent of our new members is never used because it is never discovered; and it is never discovered because no effort is made at the very beginning of their church membership to discover it. We recall Aesop's fable of how a blind man met a lame man and asked his help in crossing a stream. "I can climb upon your back," said the blind man, "and you can carry me over." "No," replied the lame man, "my legs are weak, I could not get across. But your legs are strong. You have no eyes, but I have eyes. Let me ride on *your* back and I will tell you where to step." In this manner, both succeeded in crossing. So it is in the church. If the best service is to be rendered by each member, we need to know at the beginning that individual's talents and abilities, that he may be directed aright.

There is small value for character, however, in the mere doing of things. To keep people busy merely for the sake of having them busy achieves little by way of personality development. If the doing is to make a contribution to growth, it must be accompanied by a feeling of joy and satisfaction. The convert, therefore, must be directed into that task where he can most happily express his own peculiar talents and gifts. The tasks that produce growth carry with them the interest and preference of the doer, and a sense of value in the thing done. The first demand, therefore, if we are to conserve our converts through having them share in the work of the Kingdom is that we know what our converts can do most happily, and then fit them to that task.

There is danger of the convert slipping away, if he has nothing to do. However, there is no real scarcity of worth-while tasks. Never in the history of Christianity has the church been faced with more challenging and diversified opportunities for service. The difficulty arises because of the slowness of the church in discerning those tasks and in ascertaining the abilities and preference of the convert with respect to them.

We are sensing, as never before, the responsibility of the church for the community in which it is placed. The church not only must become in itself a great character-forming force, but also the active supporter through its membership of all those agencies apart from the church which seek the community welfare. It is no commendation of the churches of a community when that community is known for its strong and flourishing religious groups, and at the same time enjoys an evil reputation for crime, vice, and drunkenness. It is difficult for a convert to live a truly Christian life in a predominantly unchristian community.

The churches cannot wash their hands of situations that corrupt our youth. Society is defiled largely because Christian men and women shut their eyes to their community responsibilities. Our churches must exercise an outreach into every aspect of home and community life—schools, business, amusements, and politics. Men and women, on coming into the churches, must be shown that they have as Christians a civic responsibility, that they are to interpret the mind of Christ and to apply it to every phase of life. In one of our cities, Christian young people circulated petitions protesting against the open crime and liquor violations which prevailed. They organized parades through the city streets. They helped to secure evidence which was placed before the authorities. As a result of their agitation, five of the worst "joints" in that city were closed.

I baptized Henry one Easter, along with a large group of other young people. For a time he seemed to be making good progress. Then we began to miss him, and rumors reached me that things were going badly with him. One morning he came to my study and said, "Pastor, I have come to ask you to have my name dropped from the church roll, for I have lost all interest in church matters." Two days previously I had been at the Old Folks' Home and had met there an old man who was blind. Suddenly it came to me that perhaps here was a way to bring cheer to the old man and, at the same time, to recover Henry. So I said: "Before we take any such action, will you do me a personal favor? Will you go to the Old Folks' Home and visit with Uncle Fred?" He looked at me in surprise, but finally he said that he would do so. He told me later what happened. The old man asked him to read the Bible to him. After Henry had complied, he put his shaky hand on Henry's knee and said, "And now, Henry, will you say a little prayer for me?" Henry was about to decline, but then he thought: "Why not? It is not for myself; I can at least do it for him." He stammered through a few sentences and left. Soon he was back in my study. His face was different and his voice was vibrant, as he said: "Pastor, never mind about removing my name. I was wrong." The rendering of a little service, in a devotional spirit, had conserved him. How we need to impress the words of our Lord upon the souls of our converts: "I have chosen you, and ordained you, that ye should go and bring forth fruit . . ." (John 15:16).

As our converts begin their Christian experience, they must come to terms with their money. This involves the way they earn it and the way they use it. If they spend one dollar a week on the movies and give twenty-five cents to the church, the measure of their growth is already decided. On such a basis they will be saying to themselves, "It is more important to support the movie industry than it is to support the kingdom of God." People give money for two reasons. One is, to support something worthy—the church, the Red Cross, the Community Chest, etc. Another and equally important reason is that they do not want to be the miserly sort of people they would inevitably become, if they kept everything for themselves. No person who always puts himself first has much chance of growing as a Christian. He can be a church member, but not a Christian.

Because the Christian spirit requires us to share with others, the utmost care should be exercised to see that every convert pledges a certain proportion of his income to God. All this should be explained to the convert prior to his uniting with the church. Pledge cards are presented as part of the reception day program. So long as the convert keeps on giving, he will keep on coming.

What is the significance of joining a church? Is it a means or an end? "A means," you reply. Yes, but many of us act as though it were an end. Statistical reports showing the large number of additions to our churches come to us frequently. These reports are an incentive to greater evangelistic effort. Unfortunately, there are no reports on the supremely important matter of convert culture. But an increased membership without corresponding spiritual growth represents dead wood instead of living timber. Everything depends upon what we do with these converts. With them lies the future of the church. To train them and hold them is our priceless privilege. All such efforts that a church puts forth will be repaid a hundredfold.

CHAPTER

9

HE WITNESSES AND IS MADE STRONG

A NUMBER OF YEARS AGO I met in the Middle West an elderly minister whom I came to know well. His character made a profound impression upon me. He had never become known as a great pulpiteer; in fact, he had spent all his ministry in a village church whose membership had never exceeded two hundred and fifty. But although his church had been small, as such things are measured, his ministry had been remarkably successful. His widespread influence had been due to his passion to multiply himself in and through his converts. It seemed that every convert he received, in the course of the years took up and personalized within himself all the noble qualities of this man of God.

In less than half a century, twenty men went out from that small church into the Christian ministry, thirteen persons went as missionaries to home and foreign fields, and twelve others became teachers in Christian educational institutions. In addition, that church sent forth numerous business and professional men and women of outstanding Christian character. A steady stream of life to reinforce the Christian witness among men! That minister's influence had been so unusual that I spent more than one afternoon with him, seeking to learn the secret of his noble ministry.

As one would expect, many factors were involved. There was his deep and continuing personal interest in each convert; there was the fact that he became their deepest confidant, the one to whom they came with all their problems; there were the classes for instruction that he gathered about him; there was the way he taught each of them to read the Bible in private devotions; there was his never-ending emphasis and watch-care in the matter of church attendance and the observance of the Lord's Supper. But the most unusual feature of his work was his class in public speech. He regularly gathered all of his converts under twenty-five years of age into this class and taught them how to express themselves easily and fearlessly. The material he used was entirely biblical. He had the class memorize great devotional Psalms and eloquent passages from the Prophets; also the Sermon on the Mount and whole chapters from the Epistles.

Two church services each year were given over to this class in expression, at which time class members recited with telling effect these mighty deliverances of the past. He conducted debates upon religious themes. "In this way," he said, "they grew so familiar with the Scriptures and with the language of religion that it became natural and easy for them to express themselves. They could pray, for both the ideas and the vocabulary of prayer were in their minds and hearts. They could speak of the things of Christ to others, because their position was so widely and openly known." Then he added this significant comment: "You know, we have underestimated the power of the tongue as a factor in building up our Christian convictions and establishing our characters." By these means he sent his converts out into the world, not hiding their gifts and not ashamed of their confession. They went forth with assurance and in command of themselves, to become Christian leaders. He equipped them to witness.

Every young convert should be taught how to use his power of speech in the service of Christ. Many are timid and must be encouraged. Many are afraid of the sound of their own voice and must learn self-mastery. Few things bring greater assurance to one's faith than to witness to it in public. This is one of God's appointed means for spiritual growth. It is Christ's will that all of His followers shall be His witnesses. In many cases it is the fault of the pastor and of the church, if these new recruits for the Kingdom never learn to speak or pray in public.

When we were planning the program for our annual New Year's Day service, one of my colleagues, in a moment of inspiration, said: "This year, why not make it a service built around prayer and witnessing? People hear enough preaching; they are getting the idea that the kingdom of God is created by sermons." Whereupon another member of the group spoke up: "It is fine to talk about a service built around prayer and witnessing, but where can you find the laymen who will conduct such a service? The average church member today does not know how to witness or to pray in public."

The criticism, I fear, was based on fact. To build a devotional service today and be certain that it will carry through, we seemingly are reduced to employing a printed liturgy and reading our prayers. People seem to be losing the gift of devotional expression. The decline of the old-time prayer meeting, with its emphasis upon spontaneous speech, has resulted in a generation of church people who have but little power in public witnessing and extemporaneous prayer. Yet that experience in expression, continuously and steadfastly expected and practiced, was a large factor in the development of Christian converts in past generations. It has become an accepted dictum of psychology that we never really know a thing until we can express it. Continuous expression deepens and fixes knowledge.

In former days the convert began his Christian life by openly stating his new-found faith before the church. Sometimes this was a cross, but he accepted it, and was established by the act. Henceforth, it was expected of him that at the church services he would witness by word of mouth to his continuing faith. If he failed to do so, the pastor with great concern would seek him out; for when the witnessing stopped he would feel certain that something was wrong. The expectancy that the converts would bear testimony, now so largely passed out of modern church life, was a mighty conserving influence. Indirectly, it was a potent force in producing Christian leaders. Six months after my conversion, my pastor in a university church came to me and said: "I have missed you at prayer meeting. We have not heard your voice for many weeks. What is the trouble?" His words brought me to self-examination, re-dedication, and a renewal of public witnessing.

I have grave doubts about the possibility of a convert being kept in power and joy, apart from some form of witnessing. While fully recognizing the basic value of the silent witness of a worthy character, I am thinking here primarily of the witness that is glorified through speech. James was discussing no superficial matter when he said: "The tongue is a little member, and boasteth great things. Behold, how great a matter a little fire kindleth!" (James 3:5).

What is speech? Whatever its function may be on its

lower levels, on its highest level it is in many respects God's chiefest endowment to man. Concerning the tongue James adds: "Therewith bless we God, even the Father" (James 3:9). Words are the instruments with which we think. Thoughts call forth words. It is equally true that words call forth thoughts. Words do more than express us; they frequently rule us. They may inflame us, misdirect us, or encourage us. It is the moral and spiritual connotation of our words that gives to human speech its startling importance.

Conversion, of course, is an indescribably personal experience. Coming to God is the most private act a man can perform. But that is only half the story. When once a man has truly found God, his Christianity can never be a mere quietism. By the very terms of his faith, each disciple is bound to be a propagandist. Our faith is not safe, nor is it real faith, unless we find it so precious that we cannot keep it to ourselves.

One of the great Christian laymen of our day tells of reaching a grave crisis in his life. Tragic happenings in his home, followed by a bitter experience with a trusted partner, had tossed his mind and heart into a maelstrom of uncertainty. He was on the verge of relinquishing his church relationship. He tells us that when he was in this state of soul, he found himself, by reason of the urging of a friend, attending the prayer meeting of his church. As the meeting progressed, the singing, the prayers, and the exposition of the Scriptures began to fill his being with a sense of quietness and peace. Presently an elderly man rose to his feet. He was known by all present as one who had recently passed through tragic, soul-shaking experiences. His wife had died under most distressing conditions. One son was serving a long term in prison. A daughter had broken away from the standards of her parents and was drifting morally. Twice his business had failed, and now, though old, he was struggling back. Yet his faith was unshaken, and the sweetness of his spirit was unmarred.

As that elderly man opened his heart in that meeting and stated once more his faith, the troubled layman, listening, felt rebuked. He said: "I knew the blackness and misery of my disappointments were as nothing to his. Suddenly, like Peter, the shame of my betrayal of my Lord by my doubts rushed over me. I had to make a confession and seek renewal." When the old gentleman had finished, he drew himself up and said: "Friends, I came here tonight a soul adrift. I had cut my moorings and was about to separate myself from my church. But the spirit of this meeting, and especially the spoken witness of our friend who has just sat down, has rebuked me and stirred me. I ask your pardon, and I ask my Lord's pardon for my waywardness of spirit; and now I pledge to Him and to you my continuing loyal devotion." He relates that he walked away from that church a renewed man, for *as he spoke,* there had come to him a strange warmness of heart and strength of spirit.

"We cannot but speak the things which we have seen and heard" (Acts 4:20). Peter was safe after Pentecost because he was bold in speech. He had been a coward and a backslider at the trial of Jesus because, when challenged as to his faith, he had kept silent. To conserve the converts, therefore, the churches must reinstate in their program something that corresponds to the old-time witnessing.

One of the most important features of John Wesley's remarkably successful program was his weekly class meetings. In them, the converts studied God's Word and bore a public witness. Their lips were unlocked in holy expression of soul convictions. Too often the lips of our converts are locked. Their inner life knows no outward flow of joyous expression. Too often we are willing to be what Clare Boothe Luce calls, "Christian coupon clippers on the original investment made by our forefathers." Yet there never has been an hour when it was easier to speak to men on matters religious. A heavyhearted world is crying for that which the Christian church alone possesses. Hungry, defeated men, finding all else turning to dust and ashes, now seek bread for their souls. If ever a Christian had an opportunity to speak out, it is today.

When the converts are young, their training in witnessing must of necessity be a very simple matter and free from all artificiality. Much of the old-time witnessing often was discounted by the unbeliever because he felt it was based upon exaggeration or was born of blind emotions. It is never convincing when a youthful Christian expresses himself in words which imitate the phraseology of a mature man. The young converts must be taught the importance of speaking simply and honestly out of their own experience.

If there is a danger of youth witnessing in an artificial, unreal manner, there is far more danger of youth never witnessing at all. In my first pastorate I had a Sunday school teacher who, realizing the importance of teaching her children to witness, had a practice of having the church members in her class witness in some way before the class at least once each month. She would say: "Children, today is our witnessing Sunday. We are taking five minutes for all who love our Lord to tell about it in just a word." Another Sunday she would say: "Next Sunday is witnessing Sunday. We want all of you who love the Lord to bring in some verse from the Bible which you have made your own through memory, or a verse from a hymn that will express what you would like to say." Sometimes she would say: "Next Sunday we want all of you who love the Lord to tell us how many boys and girls you have spoken to this week about God and your church."

This encouragement and training in witnessing was continued by this faithful teacher for many years. It is scarcely necessary to record that out of that class there came a steady stream of young converts who later became youth leaders in their church. The great thing is to establish at once in the life of the young convert the conviction that he now can witness. A candle under a bushel soon goes out. To conceal one's faith is to lose it.

There must be restored to our youth fellowship groups a larger opportunity for personal witnessing. The reading of printed slips previously assigned by the leader can never be an adequate substitute for the convert's own confession of faith, uttered in his own language. "Don't quote," said Emerson to a friend; "tell me what *you* think."

The new convert should be encouraged to become a soul winner very early in his experience. He then is like white hot metal, ready to be moulded. There should be maintained in every church a class for the training of personal workers. When a new convert unites with the church, the purpose of this class should be explained to him. A convert who early attempts this type of service will seldom fall away. Through his participation in personal evangelism, he will gain an insight into the meaning of the whole Kingdom enterprise which will command his loyalty down through the years.

Some years ago I baptized a young man who seemed to be endowed with ability above the average. Because of his deep sincerity I coveted him for some type of Christian service. When he had turned in his personal data sheet, expressing his preference in service, he had not mentioned evangelism. But I felt that in that way he could be greatly useful among the youth of the congregation. So I sat down with him and explained the nature and importance of such work, and he readily volunteered for it. He joined the personal workers' class which met at 6:30 each Sunday evening. At the end of eight weeks, he was paired with an experienced older man and began the actual work of contact evangelism. From the start, God richly blessed his efforts. He came to me on the following Sunday, his face radiant, to tell of his experience in winning to Christ one of his companions. He continued his efforts. Within a year he had won a dozen young people to Christ. In a later conference, he said, "Pastor, what does one have to possess to be a minister of Christ?" For nearly fifteen years now he has been an honored minister of the gospel. This young man grew in Christian character, and ultimately he entered the Christian ministry, because he had been enlisted in evangelism. A few years ago he said to me, "When I won my first soul to Christ, I knew at once that I had to be a minister."

The best way for a Christian to keep his religion up to the mark is by sharing it with another. Young converts make excellent soul winners, for they are concerned; and it is concern, more than knowledge, that brings people to God. We should give the new Christian the joy of spiritual service. All too frequently the convert's buoyant desire to serve the Lord is channeled by the church into the kitchen, into serving tables, or into some other secondary field. He could do such work in a lodge, a club, or any such institution, without the necessity of

his conversion. Since he has come into the church because
of his desire to invest his life in spiritual things, let us
not belittle him by filling his hands with chaff instead
of with seed for sowing. Let us get him started saving
others, seeking them out with words of sincere, kindly
testimony as to Christ's power to save. In seeking others
with prayerful concern, he will both save them and establish his own Christian faith.

Following Easter, when the number of accessions had
been large, I at times gave that Easter group a special
name, as in a high school or college, calling them, for
example, the Class of 1940. I tried to cultivate in each
Easter class a sense of relationship to the group, and to
build up on the part of the members a warm fellowship.
For the first year, such a class met once each month. The
meeting sometimes was held at the church; more often
in a home. We would go over the roll together to discover
if any were missing from church attendance or were
failing to participate in church activities. The members
took upon themselves the work of visiting such and lend-
ing encouragement. They assumed a definite responsibility for one another. The group canvassed avenues of
outreach, prepared prospect lists, and assigned the names
of visitors. Prayer was offered for the visitors and for
the prospects. The effectiveness of this effort was amaz-
ing. At the close of a year, one such class reported that
every member was actively engaged in some form of
church service. The class of the previous year won fourteen people to Christ and the church, and they themselves,
through their witnessing, were established in the faith.

James Boswell, in his memorable biography of Samuel
Johnson, tells that Johnson spent all his days under the
shadow of one stupendous text which hung over him like
a daily judgment. The text was, "Unto whomsoever much

is given, of him shall be much required" (Luke 12:48). Who can measure the responsibility that is ours to make the facts of the gospel known? To fix that sense of deep responsibility in the consciousness of the new convert is to go far toward making him a true churchman.

There is immeasurable value in expressing our deepest convictions to those about us. Many of us may admire the strong, silent type of person of whom the Vermont farmer has become the type. But it was too long a silence which that Vermont farmer broke when he said to his wife: "Do you know, Sarah, you have meant so much to me that sometimes it is almost more than I can stand, not to tell you about it." Most of us have gone too long without telling those whom we contact daily how much Christ means to us, and how much He can mean to them.

Each year at Harvard Commencement a baccalaureate hymn, containing these stanzas, is sung:

"Let children learn the mighty deeds
Which God performed of old,
Which, in our younger years, we saw,
And which our fathers told.

"Our lips shall tell them to our sons,
And they again to theirs,
That generations yet unborn
May teach them to their heirs."

—*Psalm 78, metrical version*

To establish that sense of trusteeship in the hearts and minds of the converts entering the church is one of our primary tasks. To bear witness is to establish the soul.

10

HE GROWS AND IS GLORIFIED

THE EVER-PRESENT NOTE of hope for all of us is the inner urge to grow and develop. In all this world there is nothing more beautiful than growth. When does a person pass his prime? Physically perhaps at forty, mentally perhaps in the middle fifties; but spiritually he need never stop growing. As soon as a person finds his best years in the yesterday of his spiritual experience, the mark of "finis" is upon him. But so long as he is growing spiritually, he bears the marks of youth.

We are troubled by the realization that we are growing old physically. Not many of us possess the courageous spirit of Robert Browning, who represents Rabbi Ben Ezra as saying:

> "Grow old along with me!
> The best is yet to be,
> The last of life, for which the first was made."

But what about our spirituality? Are we as eager to keep growing spiritually as we are to keep young physically? Think how much of the world's misery would be checked, if at seventy our ideals were higher than they were at twenty!

The growing Christian life blossoms out into beauty. No living thing, whether violet or arbutus, whether oak

93

or pine, can fulfill the law of its growth without at last coming into loveliness. The bulb is ugly, but if it obeys its urge to grow it will flower into all the tulip's brilliance. The sweetbriar at first is only a thorny bush, but if it develops steadily it will suddenly gleam with pink or white blossoms.

Whoever obeys the laws of his work will find beauty as its crown. Obey the laws of speech and you have eloquence. Obey the laws of form and color and you have an art masterpiece. Obey the laws of the Divine will and you have adorned and made beautiful the doctrine of God our Savior. When once a genuine convert obeys fully the laws of development and spiritual growth written deep in his nature, you have the loveliest thing on earth—a redeemed and glorified personality.

We are in the world to grow and yet to grow. Jesus came to fill the soul with noble discontent. Nothing is static after His spirit has been received. Each victory marks only a spot where the disciple sets up his tent for the night, to march forward upon the morrow to new achievements.

Being a Christian is a process of growing. There is a sense, as Martin Luther pointed out, in which a person never is, but is always becoming, a Christian. Growing every day more familiar with Jesus' life, more loyal to His spirit and ideals, more swift to respond to His will, more loving, more kind, more unselfish in all our human relations! As Dr. Sockman has so well emphasized: "It is one thing to commit oneself to Christ as Lord and Master; it is another to bring all the interests of life into subjection to Him. And here is the point where so many of us fall short of being Christian. We have never brought the whole of ourselves into subjection to Christ. Some of us are converted in will but not in taste. We want to do what is right, but we do not like to do it. . . . We long for the kingdom of God to come, but we are not willing to pay for it. Some of us are converted in our appetites but not in our politics. We control our lusts but vote our prejudices. Ah, this business of becoming a Christian requires long and patient discipline."[1]

It is, then, a wondrous, thrilling, beautiful thing to grow. And there is a message which each generation needs to hear; namely, that "it is better further on." That "it doth not yet appear what we shall be." That "the glory of this latter house shall be greater than of the former." That it will be "sweeter as the years go by." The Christian life starts out on earth, it soon gets to the mountain peaks. Then, in dreams and visions, it soars beyond the mountains to the stars. Although "it doth not yet appear what we shall be," to grow into that experience is the very purpose of our being. From this point of view, the work of saving men involves all the long process by which a worthy personality is achieved. To be saved is to develop a life so worth while in this world that it will be worth extending for that longer while called eternity.

The basic fact to which we are repeatedly brought back is that spiritual conservation and growth are fundamentally a matter of sustaining right spiritual attitudes within. Paul writes, "the inward man is renewed day by day" (2 Cor. 4:36). In another letter he writes that we must be "strengthened with might by his Spirit in the inner man" (Eph. 3:16). There is, then, an inner life for the Christian. It must be revitalized and fostered continuously by the Holy Spirit. It is there that we find the Holy of Holies of the Christian religion. The apostle

[1] From *Now to Live!*, by Ralph W. Sockman. Copyright, 1946, Stone and Pierce. Used by permission of Abingdon-Cokesbury Press.

reminds us that "if any man be in Christ, he is a new creature: old things are passed away; behold, all things are become new." It is the Spirit who brings us into the presence of God. The Spirit transforms the whole being, the entire outlook, the very quality of the life.

The indwelling Spirit of God, who comes to us in the hour of our surrender to Christ, continues with us as our abiding guest, a creative agent in us and through us. His power to recreate us and to change our habits and conduct will be determined by our attitude toward Him. One suspects that the major reason for the many spiritual cripples among us is that so many of us have continually grieved and insulted the Spirit that dwells within us. We do not permit Him to direct our lives. We do not allow Him to work His way in our hearts. When we thus quench and grieve the Spirit, He can do no mighty works in us or through us. Our lives become powerless. On the other hand, if our lives are yielded to Him, there is nothing that can defeat or crush us.

Will the Holy Spirit stay with our converts? He will, unless driven away. If the convert will let Him have full sway, duty will become a delight. The spirit of indifference and coldness will disappear before the flame of His presence. Many of our converts soon become dull, heavyhearted, and burdened with a consciousness of defeat. If the Spirit of God is given a chance, He will change all that. He will put a song on their lips and in their hearts. He will turn discouragement into encouragement, praying into prevailing.

The Holy Spirit builds the inner life of the Christian. He is the originator and the sustainer of all spiritual growth. All external devices and organizations, such as clubs, classes, agencies, sociability, recreation, and study, are good when His presence is welcomed into the heart of the believer, but largely futile when He is absent. "Not by might, nor by power, but by my spirit, saith the Lord of hosts" (Zech. 4:6).

The tremendously significant thing about the Holy Spirit is that He can change people whenever they really want to be changed. He can smash the evil habits of the convert and nurture his spiritual growth until his life becomes marked with lines of beauty. He can change one's disposition. With His help, we can move up to a better life. If we tell Him that we want a better life, and mean it, we can have that better life.

In his *Book of Prayers, Written for Use in an Indian College*, John S. Hoyland has included this prayer that we all might well make our own:

"Lover of our souls,
  Thou knowest our inmost being,
  Thou seest in us the desires and motives,
  Which we ourselves cannot clearly descry.

"Thou knowest what powers for love and for service
  Thou hast set in our souls;
  Thou knowest every possibility of perfect manhood
  Which lieth here asleep.

"Father,
  Take into thy rich store-house,
  Every noble impulse, every high ideal,
  Every right faculty, every capacity for love that is within us.

"Though here our true selves may never be realised,
  Yet keep and use in thine own good time our powers for love and
    for goodness:
  Add them to thy spiritual resources,
  Pour them into thy secret reservoirs,
  Whence all the nations of the earth,
  Which now lie parched and desolate,
  Shall some day be refreshed and restored with thy water of life."[2]

[2] From *Book of Prayers, Written for Use in an Indian College*, by John S. Hoyland. Published by The Challenge, London, 1921. Used by permission.

CHAPTER

11

THE LAPSED CHURCH MEMBER CAN BE RECOVERED

AT THE BEGINNING of a pastorate in New England, I discovered a strange apathy toward evangelism. It was due, partly, to the unusually large number of inactive members whose names were carried on the church roll. "Why should we seek new members when, in previous evangelistic efforts, we merely took in a lot of people whom we never see and who never support our work?" That feeling was expressed again and again. The officers of the church were doing nothing to recover those lapsed members; instead, they were using them as an excuse for their own indolence in seeking further expansion. My words come back to me now: "Forget them for the present. Let us go after new converts to take their place." We did just that, and the church soon was doing a marvelous job in outreach. We saw so many new faces that we forgot our lapsed members.

But I was wrong. I have learned better with the passing of the years. The church has a responsibility for those who have united with its fellowship that cannot be thus lightly brushed aside, for the major cause of lapsed members all too frequently is found in the life of the church itself.

What minister has not heard some church officer say: "Why don't we drop their names? What's the use of carrying a lot of dead timber? They never come. They never give a dollar. They have no interest in our church. Let us clean house." We admit, of course, that there are many cases where little can be done. But to take the easy way and say, "We are through," is too often a reflection, not of our understanding, but of our spiritual laziness and lack of compassion.

These cases are difficult. It has become proverbial that it is easier to win a convert than to restore a backslider. But the fact remains that lapsed members can be restored. The church that will patiently, prayerfully, and sacrificially give itself to this endeavor, will behold marvelous recoveries. No church is warranted in lightly cutting away any member from the body of our Lord. May I offer a few suggestions which I have found to be practically helpful in this matter.

First, *make a careful list of those in the church membership who have not been attending public worship.* Include in this list the names of all members who have not attended at least once in three months. That is being generous, surely. These names should be listed, for full information cannot be retained by memory. A careful study should then be made of each case. What are the circumstances surrounding the member which might have contributed to his lapse? What of his home? his occupation? his recreation? his friendships? his habits? When these matters have been explored, it often will be found that his absence is in a measure justifiable.

For six months I sat in judgment upon one of my members who in that period had never appeared at church. Then I bethought me that I had no right to judge without information. So, belatedly, I sought him out. I discovered that his wife was ill, and that it was her illness which had prevented his coming. His daughter, who cared for her mother on weekdays, had a Sunday job; consequently, on that day he had the full care of his wife. Because the wife's illness was of a mental nature, he had sought to conceal it. The good man had been censured when he should have been receiving help from the sympathetic and understanding members of his church.

In another case, nearly two years passed before the absence of one of our members received serious consideration. Then in a board meeting someone spoke up: "Better drop his name; he has lost interest in the church." So I went around to see this "lapsed" brother. It was on a Sunday afternoon. I ascertained from his wife, who was a member of another church, that for a long time his job had required him to work on Sunday. His work was of a necessary nature. Yet none of us had been aware of it, and he had been unjustly criticized. When we set up on Wednesday evening a service of worship designed especially for Sunday workers, he, with others so situated, gladly came and participated in it.

Two brothers, thirteen and fifteen years of age, were baptized on the same day. For two months they attended Sunday school and church regularly. Then they stopped coming. At the end of the year the Sunday school superintendent and the deacons said: "It was a mistake to baptize those boys. They have lost all interest. They have dropped out of Sunday school." So they were tagged "lapsed." One evening I went around to look them up. I found them at home studying. They were upstanding young fellows. Then I discovered that nine months before, their mother, who had supported the home, had lost her job through ill health, and that much of the home support had devolved upon these two sons. One had taken a job in a hotel for Saturdays and Sundays. The other was employed as an assistant to the janitor and watchman in a large factory, and this work took his entire week end. I felt like apologizing to those boys. We had been doing them a grave injustice. When our Youth Fellowship developed a half-hour worship service, held in the chapel on Monday evenings, both boys came on invitation and thereafter regularly attended those services.

The first step, therefore, in the recovery of those who have lapsed in the matter of attending public worship is to acquaint ourselves with the conditions surrounding each case. This is necessary, if we are to judge fairly and to approach each individual with an open mind and a kindly heart. The church member or minister who approaches lapsed members in a critical spirit will utterly fail. The best approach is one of love, kindness, and deep concern—a genuine concern that reflects the concern of God lest one of His followers should drift away. When we have made such a close investigation of the circumstances surrounding our lapsed members, we may discover to our joy that many of them have not lapsed at all. Instead of judgment, they likely have needed the sympathetic help of their church.

Yet, with due charity exercised, it will be found that beyond all such cases there remain many who have actually disassociated themselves from the church. Here again the most careful collecting of information is needed. Have you ascertained the reason why they are no longer active members? Did they take offense at something that was said? Was it because of a lack of sociability among the members? Was it because of a dislike of the preacher? Of the choir? Was it because of financial limitations?

Was it because of domestic difficulties? Was it due to outside influences, such as worldly associations? Was it due to bad habits—drink, gambling, or loose morals? Seek to discover the real reason for the lapse. When your recovery organization moves into action, its work will be effective only to the extent that information of this sort is available.

Second, *make a list of those who have lapsed in the matter of contributing toward the support of the church.* When we recall that only 50 per cent of the members of the average church are givers of record to the current expense fund, and that only 30 per cent are givers of record to the missionary budget, it is evident that every church is carrying on its roll many members who have lapsed financially. Many, of course, did not begin to give systematically when they united with the church. But others, having once begun, soon ceased to contribute. Few churches ever measure up to their financial potential.

Consequently, ascertain and make a record of the reasons why these members stopped giving, or why they never began to give. Some may tell you that they were never asked to give. But why have some who started giving, stopped? Did the member lose his job? Was his income reduced? Did he incur unusual expenses, such as might be caused by prolonged illness, misfortune in business, the education of his children, or buying a new home? This information is to be secured, not as a basis for criticism, but as a guide to an intelligent and sympathetic approach. You cannot talk helpfully to such a man unless you know his situation and circumstances.

Third, *having carefully studied and classified the lapsed members, how shall we proceed with a program of recovery?* I am persuaded that the answer is to be found within the realm of an enlarged and deepened spiritual fellowship. Friendship is still the mightiest force in social and neighborhood relations. Many of these folks came to our churches in search of that which they had enjoyed in the village or country church where they were converted—the spirit of friendship. If they find it in the church which they have joined, they will remain active in that church. If they sense its absence, they all too often will look for that fellowship among the non-churched.

I have discovered that many of our lapsed members can be won back through a well organized and directed neighborhood zone program. Let me describe its operation. I found that on three near-by streets, there were six families who seemingly had broken away from our church fellowship. Every appeal made to them to return to worship and to service had failed. They were completely indifferent, and two of them had become bitter. But in that neighborhood we had also ten families of earnest, devoted church workers. I asked one of these families to open its home and to invite the heads of the other nine families to an evening of fellowship.

When opportunity came, I congratulated those present upon the fine evening of Christian fellowship, told them how much such gatherings could mean to our church, and what a force they could be in the work of Christian outreach in the community. Then I told them that in their immediate neighborhood there were six families which, although on our church roll, had lost all interest in our church. Some of them had found friendships in lodges or clubs; others had set up imaginary barriers between themselves and our church. But nominally they were still connected with our church, and we had a responsibility under God for them and their homes. Then I spoke of the factors that keep one in the church, emphasizing particularly the spirit of fellowship. "It is evident," I said, "that these people did not find that sort of warm-hearted fellowship in our church. Otherwise, they would not have left us,"

Then I challenged the group to encompass those six homes with friendly interest, good will, and fellowship. I asked them to plan a home fellowship hour once each month, such as they had enjoyed that evening. They were not to approach those six homes as a church group; neither were they to solicit their return to the church. At first, they were simply to contact them and invite them as neighbors to the fellowship group. One family we never did reach. They had become cynical with respect to life in general. But within a year, five of those lapsed families were attending the neighborhood fellowship group, and were back at worship in the church. When the financial canvass was made, being interested in their church once more, they pledged their support. Three of the women united with our woman's organization and two of the men became active on our boards. Out of those six lapsed homes thirteen children returned to Sunday school. It is my conviction that through the development of such a neighborhood group plan 90 per cent of our lapsed members can be won to active participation in the church program.

Christian homes are our greatest asset, yet for the most part they are not being employed in Christian service. We must make the fellowship among church members so superior to that found elsewhere—so superior in warmth, unselfish interest, and helpfulness—that the church members will prize it above all associations outside the church. This means endless effort, unselfish use of our home facilities, careful planning of evening programs, and aggressive promotion. But the church that is willing to pay this price can recover most of its lapsed members.

If a man does not give regularly to his church, it is useless to scold and harangue him. A man gives only as he perceives values in return for his investment—values in worship, evangelism, education, world outreach, fellowship. But if his heart is cold toward the church, he is blind to all such values. To secure his financial co-operation, therefore, we had better forget about his money. We should begin on the level where he is interested and where he finds enjoyment; that is, in the realm of fellowship.

It is futile to suppose that those who have left us can be won back to church attendance and support merely by pressure invitations or by dissertations on duty. We should frankly face this fact. These people are not coming back by reason of any such urging. Those who love our Lord and His church must be willing to pay the price; they must demonstrate in both their personal life and their home life a sincere fellowship toward all who come among them. "Brethren, if a man be overtaken in a fault, ye which are spiritual, restore such an one in the spirit of meekness; considering thyself, lest thou also be tempted" (Gal. 6:1).

Fourth, *We may recover many of our lapsed members through the discovery and use of their talents*. Talents which we in the church do not note or use, organizations outside the church are quick to observe and employ. Two boys of exceptional musical talent joined our church. But apparently we had no place in which we could use them. We had neither an orchestra nor a youth chorus. Soon I began to miss these boys from Sunday school. Three months went by. On inquiry, I found that they had joined a dance orchestra, and that they were rehearsing

on Sunday mornings. We appealed to them to come back
to Sunday school and church. But they did not come. It
seemed we had lost them. I was deeply concerned. Then
a good layman, with whom I had discussed the problem,
said: "Why can't we have an orchestra in our church?
I will back it to the extent of $200." We decided to
approach those two fine boys. This layman arranged for
a lunch for the four of us, and we sat and talked together. Would they come and organize and conduct such
an orchestra? Within a week they had assented. What
a job they did! Both boys were back in the church. And
both, with the passing of the years, have become splendid Christian leaders.

In the depth of the great depression, our church faced
a financial crisis. Staggering under a church debt, we
found our income insufficient to carry our program. The
financial leadership in the church had fallen down badly.
The church officials seemed incapable of dealing with
the situation. Where could we find a man who could
give us guidance during those trying days? Then, one
day at lunch, I was reminded by one of our members
that the man who was heading up most of the charitable
drives in the community was a member of our church,
though he had not been inside of it for four years. He
was a quiet man who would never push himself forward.
He had joined our church, and when nothing had been
offered him to do along the line of his peculiar talents,
he had quietly dropped out, to be picked up by the charitable organizations of the community. I had never seen
him in church; in fact, he had become almost forgotten.
It was a happy moment for the church, and for that man
as well, when one of the men at the table said: "If we
could get Mr. B. to head up our finances, he could lead
us out of our difficulty." "Why not?" I said. "Have you

tried to enlist him?" They had not. So we went to see him. We placed the situation fully and frankly before him, and asked him for the investment of his talent in behalf of the church. Three days later he agreed to serve. Then began a wonderful experience for our church and for that man. Within six months the church had made a remarkable recovery. But what was equally important, that quiet, earnest, highly gifted man now sat each Sunday in his church—worshiping. Both he and his family were recovered to the church.

Fifth, *I would suggest that sometimes a bit of heartbreak may help in recovery.* I know a pastor who has been unusually successful in this matter of restoration. When he visits those of his people who have lapsed, he shows such genuine concern, such depth of sorrow because of their indifference, such agonizing in prayer in their behalf, that God has used him again and again to soften their hearts and to reawaken their interest. Somebody must be deeply and sacrificially concerned for these lapsed brethren, and that concern must be *shown.*

We give up too quickly and too easily. The easy way out of the situation—but not the Christian way—is to cut off the lapsed members and be rid of them. But no church can thus lightly escape its responsibility. When once the church has received a convert into its membership, it must accept and thereafter discharge the task of developing in that convert a mature Christian character; and should one of these converts go astray, the church with watchfulness, patience, and prayer must do all in its power to recover that member.

This spirit and this purpose were beautifully and impressively displayed by the apostle Paul, who in his letter to the Christians in Rome, wrote: "For I long to see you, that I may impart unto you some spiritual gift, to the

end ye may be established" (Rom. 1:11). And we ourselves, none too sure of our own strength, are included
in the prayer of the apostle Peter: "But the God of all
grace, who hath called us unto his eternal glory by Christ
Jesus, after that ye have suffered a while, make you
perfect, stablish, strengthen, settle you. To him be glory
and dominion for ever and ever. Amen" (1 Pet. 5:10-11).